WOUNDED EAGLE

The Politically Correct Seduction of the Law in Kentucky

COL (Ret) John W. Smith

ISBN 978-1-64140-034-3 (paperback)
ISBN 978-1-64140-035-0 (digital)

Christian Faith Publishing, Inc.
832 Park Avenue
Meadville, PA 16335
www.christianfaithpublishing.com

Printed in the United States of America

This journal is dedicated to the thousands of Youth ChalleNGe cadre, staff, and administrators throughout our great nation. The daily efforts each perform toward creating change in that group of at-risk youth willing to accept the challenge is undoubtedly one of the best-kept secrets in America.

I especially dedicate this book to those members of the Bluegrass and Appalachian ChalleNGe Academies. Many of our graduates are so very proud of their accomplishments and sound out that "ChalleNGe Me!" with a vigor and pride only this singular experience can instill.

To 1SG Burgess, Ms Graves, MSG Onusko, PSG Carthen, and PSG Windom, I am proud to have shared just a few of your many years of accomplishment and the adversity of our single unjust allegation.

To the many who have encouraged me and have read and recommended changes to this journal and my attempt in expressing my heart through the somewhat technical nature of the content, thank you so very much.

CONTENTS

Section IV. Extrajudicial Circumstances

Appendixes

PROLOGUE

Justice will not be served until those who are unaffected are as outraged as those who are.

—Benjamin Franklin

Bugles, bells, and the bailiff's call have sounded, demanding my response to the call for action. I have answered that call against tyrants on sandy battlefields, against the lack of discipline and scholastic confidence in our youth, and finally against an unjust allegation in our Federal Court. This journal recounts part of that final struggle; may it become your clarion call to action!

We all strive to create a legacy that is more sunshine than mist, more good than evil, more uplifting than demeaning. The English Wesleyan minister William Lonsdale Watkinson first printed the following expression in 1907: "But denunciatory rhetoric is so much easier and cheaper than good works, and proves a popular temptation. Yet is it far better to light the candle than to curse the darkness." Most of the symbolic mountains I have climbed in my life have been pure adversity. With the help of many exemplary teams, I have reached the summit of each mountain, and each effort has resulted in personal growth and achievement. I have proceeded from one career to another feeling that my previous accomplishments in life were developmental and I should not sit to consider my laurels. I wanted to share and give back some of what God had given me. I have recently experienced the denunciatory rhetoric fueled by popular temptation, being dragged down to seemingly culminate in a pit of castigation. At the apparent end of my managerial involvement, others tried to extinguish my candle with much alleged darkness. I refuse to allow my final body of service, and the distinguished work of those who have helped me, be smothered forever! This book is my effort to relight a candle for each of them so their good works continue to light the way for others.

From late 2014 through mid-2016, I was the object of focus of our federal justice system relating to the performance of my duties as director of Bluegrass ChalleNGe Academy. I never imagined I would ever be forced to endure these difficulties during my career in the military or during my service to Youth ChalleNGe. What follows is an explanation of what each of us may face, if and when those with an agenda and an opportunity determine to use any of us for their purpose. I will attempt to lay out this story as it occurred, and summarize the warnings at the conclusion.

While Benjamin Franklin and our other founding fathers were a fraternity of citizens who not only lived with and grappled with the forces of tyranny and divided loyalties among the colonists, they were also a body of men fighting to define and deliver our new nation into democratic ideals of liberty, justice, and freedom under the protection of law.

As a recent defendant under federal prosecution for an alleged misdemeanor, I have become acutely aware of how our current system of American justice has evolved. It is my hope this discussion causes you to examine the works and opinions of justices, scholars, and other authors regarding their views and recommendations to improve our system of justice. Regrettably, after you read this journal, you will find that our system of justice has become a completely adversarial process, where prosecutors and attorneys maneuver through legal tactics to gain any advantage, regardless of the justice, the law, or the truths involved.

Americans of good character, and dedicated public servants in particular, work to insure their actions and efforts are consistently and exactly on the right side of the line separating justice and injustice in the performance of their assigned tasks. In the governmental sector, there is absolutely no incentive or benefit to be gained by marginalization of correct actions. Public servants reap no special rewards for inaction in cases of potential subordinate criminal actions. They, like all Americans, can only act on the law and policy they have been trained to execute and implement. No celestial process allows any of us to perceive the many thousands of laws that are published in the many statutory and administrative, though often hidden, places. The search for these innumerable locations would mean that we would continuously search for, and only seldom find, applicable requirements. These continuous search activities would likely be fruitless and allow us no time to perform those tasks our employers and the public expect and mandate us to perform.

While we can never recite each law and regulation, each American grasps the symbolism incorporated into the depiction of Lady Justice, a symbol since Roman times, representing in a fair, balanced, sacred and universal set of rules guiding the United States Justice System. Each of us fears involvement in the judicial system, but we naively assume that the truth of any issue will prevail within any given case. Recently, I was made well-aware of just how Lady Justice is indeed a blindfolded matriarch in this country. I found her more like a blinded operator at the wheel of a steamroller, all too ready to crush the lives of the innocent instead of standing guard at the entrance to the courthouse to insure justice prevails for all. After my experience with our federal judicial system, I wonder if Lady Justice should face the courthouse with sword in hand, instead of facing the people. In late 2014 through 2016, I, and others indicted with me, felt the impact and the injustice of our federal justice system. These few chapters are but a short chronology of what happened and what I have discovered and experienced relating to our current system.

The ambiguity and scope of our laws, statutes, and regulations far exceed anyone's ability to identify, understand, and respond. Even our government agents cannot meet the requirements to support and train identified agencies regarding their responsibilities. Glenn Harlan Reynolds shared a grim truth as he writes,[1]

---

[1] Glenn Harlan Reynolds, "'You are probably breaking the law right now'," *USA Today*, March 29, 2015.

"'Regulatory crimes' of this sort are incredibly numerous and a category that is growing quickly. They are the ones likely to trap unwary individuals into being felons without knowing it. That is why Michael Cottone, in a just-published Tennessee Law Review article, suggests that maybe the old presumption that individuals know the law is outdated, unfair and maybe even unconstitutional. 'Tellingly,' he writes, 'no exact count of the number of federal statutes that impose criminal sanctions has ever been given, but estimates from the last 15 years range from 3,600 to approximately 4,500.' Meanwhile, according to recent congressional testimony, the number of federal regulations (enacted by administrative agencies under loose authority from Congress) carrying criminal penalties may be as many as 300,000.

And it gets worse. While the old-fashioned common law crimes typically required a culpable mental state—you had to realize you were doing something wrong — the regulatory crimes generally don't require any knowledge that you're breaking the law. This seems quite unfair. As Cottone asks, 'How can people be expected to know all the laws governing their conduct when no one even knows exactly how many criminal laws exist?'"

There is a time when the sheer numbers of laws overwhelm us, when we follow known law only to be accused in our ignorance of unknown law. On these occasions, our only hope is that prosecutorial discretion will save us. We expect the just prosecutor to discover that we did everything we knew to do, and that if we indeed did violate any law, it was because no one had shared this law with us. Surely, he or she will resist any charge against us, provide the required training, and fully explain the consequences of inaction, and possibly the resources available to us to help us perform our duties. Sometimes the process works this way; however, too frequently the prosecutors are motivated to charge an individual for their politics, their ethnicity, to execute a personal agenda, in order to fulfill a quota, or just because the nature of the alleged offense assures a win. In these cases, otherwise innocent people learn that the law is the law and that ignorance is no excuse. Not amusingly, some government officials who break the law do get to plead ignorance and good intentions, under the doctrine of good faith "qualified immunity." We were proof that "qualified immunity" is not provided to lower-level former government officials!

The subject case of this journal involves proceedings where five of my staff and I were involved in is based on a "strict liability" statute. In these types of cases, the prosecution, with the consent of the court, does not have to prove that the defendant had any knowledge that their actions or inactions were improper or that there was even intent to do wrong. According to Laurie L. Levenson's introduction in a Cornell Law Review paper,[2] the concept of strict liability can be defined in the following manner:

"For years, courts and commentators have struggled with the criminal strict liability doctrine. It is a doctrine that contradicts the most basic principles of modem criminal law. Ordinarily, a criminal offense requires both a voluntary act (actus reus) and a culpable state of mind (mens rea). Strict liability permits the conviction of a criminal defendant in the absence of mens rea. In ignoring the defendants intent, the strict liability doctrine even allows for punishment of individuals who, because of deception, unwittingly commit prohibited acts. Not surprisingly, many scholars are critical of the doctrine. Commenting on the imposition of liability without regard to the defendants state of mind, Professor Kadish stated, 'If a principle is at work here, it is the principle of 'tough luck.'

Yet, arguments against criminal strict liability have not convinced everyone. In particular, prosecutors and legislators welcome the use of strict liability crimes. Convictions are more easily obtained if the prosecution need not prove a culpable mental state. Intent, often the most difficult issue to prove, must be shown indirectly from a defendants statements and conduct. Application of criminal strict liability relieves the state of this burden. The strict liability doctrine affords both an efficient and nearly guaranteed way to convict defendants.

---

[2]   Laurie L. Levenson, "Good Faith Defense: Reshaping Strict Liability Crimes," *Cornell Law Review*, Volume 78, Issue 3 March 1993, Article 2. http://scholarship.law.cornell.edu/cgi/viewcontent.cgi?article=2482&context=clr

Caught in the middle of this dispute are the trial courts. While judges wish to uphold legislative intent and enforce the laws as enacted, they must also confront, face-to-face, individual strict liability defendants for whom punishment simply is not warranted. Trial judges may find it hard to imprison, even for a short period, a person who has not committed a crime intentionally.

Presently, the strict liability doctrine operates as an irrebuttable presumption. Once an individual is shown to have committed an impermissible act, the law presumes some level of culpable intent justifying punishment. This basic presumption, however, is not always valid. Sometimes a defendant will face several years in jail despite having taken extraordinary efforts to comply with the law. In these situations, the irrebuttable presumption will unjustly convict an individual who is not criminally culpable. Because the defendant took all reasonable preventive steps and was still unaware of the unlawful nature of his conduct, traditional purposes of punishment would not be served by prosecuting this individual."

Please consider the recent testimony of our Director of the Federal Bureau of Investigation, as it relates to the "irrebuttable presumption" identified above, when he testified before Congress in 2016 that each indictment recommended by the FBI requires that the individual knew they were breaking the law. The requirement Director Comey recounted does not seem to apply in the Western District of Kentucky.

As you consider the implications for the common man regarding what has happened to a few dedicated public servants in this case, please consider the thoughts of Supreme Court Justice Antonin Scalia, when he quoted the 1753 comments of Sir William Blackstone from his Of the Nature of Laws in General; stating, "Not like Caligula, who (according to Dio Cassius) wrote his laws in a very small character, and hung them up upon high pillars, the more effectually to ensnare the people."

SECTION I

The Man and
the Mission

1

JOHN WAYNE SMITH:
THE FORMATIVE YEARS

A good name is to be chosen rather than great
riches, loving favor rather than silver or gold.

—Proverbs 22: 1

I have enjoyed a life of work, education, family, worship, and love.
There are high expectations in each of these areas, instilled in each of
us by parents, family, teachers, mentors, and close friends.

My mother, Mary Alice Brindle Smith, was a very capable, determined, and humble Midwestern lady. She was the second daughter
of Charles L. and Vesta Brindle, though her sister Margaret died at
a very early age. George was the older brother Mom depended upon
for sibling guidance and protection. Chet was the younger brother
whom Mom adored and who could do no wrong. Mom's mother,
Vesta, passed just after Mom had completed high school. Mom was
nineteen, full of dreams and opportunity, and dedicated herself to
filling the role of her mother in the home. Over the next eleven years,
she cared for, fed, and doctored her father and brothers. She became

the bookkeeper for the family's early hybrid seed corn business and ran errands to keep the business going. During her few times of leisure, she enjoyed fishing with her friends and participating in the Daffodil Rebekah Lodge. Here she later attained the designation of Past Noble Grand. Both George and Chet served in World War II. You can only imagine the difficult nights Grandpa Charles and Mom shared, after long days keeping the family farm and business going, during this time. Mom also served as a Sunday school teacher in her native Union, Iowa. In 1949, Mom's father experienced an injury-related stomach ulcer bleed that took his life. This was a life-changing event in Mom's life.

My father, Bronvil McRoyal Smith, was an outgoing, hard-charging Kentuckian. He was the second child of Clarence McRoyal Smith and Delilah Mae Bradley Smith. His immediate family included five sisters and two brothers. He grew up involved in agriculture and construction work. Dad had experienced poor eyesight from an early age. When World War II began, he was denied enlistment on multiple occasions. He was finally accepted in 1945, having completed his basic training and medical assistant training just before the war ended. He reenlisted a year after being discharged after the conclusion of the war and served for a period in Berlin, Germany, as a circulating operating room attendant (I think). When he returned from this period of service, Dad answered the call of relatives, the Bradley family, living in Union, Iowa, to assist with their farming activities. It was during this time that my father met my mother, and soon after the death of Mom's father, they were wed at the "Little Brown Church in the Vale" at Nashua, Iowa. During this year, the family decided to sell the family farm as siblings wanted to pursue individual interests. I was born in Eldora, Iowa, on November 24, 1950. I was brought home from the doctor's office and lived in an upstairs room of our family's two-story craftsman home in Union, Iowa. I was six weeks old when we moved back to my father's home in Kentucky. On a visit to Iowa in 2007, we were invited into that first home by the current owners. My mother described the earlier functions of all rooms of the house. Upon entering an upstairs room with a distinctive outside wall, my mother went to the windows, gazed out at the cornfields, and exclaimed to me, "This is the room you were brought home to from the doctor's office." It was a very profound moment for me. I am so very happy to have had this moment with my mother. LaDonna and I haven't done that with our children yet, but we should!

My early memories are of family gatherings, the love of my mother, and of school. I think my childhood was as much like any other child born in the 1950s, filled with the same activities and expectations. Sunday afternoons were spent with our Smith grandparents, enjoying every great meal prepared by my grandmother. The Smith kin seemed to gather there quite often, and we enjoyed the stories, card games, and croquet contests that were always played on the summer lawn.

Dad was involved in many endeavors at this time. He constructed the Three Forks Feed Mill, with family help, and made it a viable business. My grandfather really enjoyed the companionship of the local farmers who frequented the mill, and he and my father negotiated a trade between the mill and the approximately 360 acres of rolling hills and river bottom land in Three Forks. Dad also decided to be among the first agricultural and commercial heavy equipment service providers in our area. He purchased a Caterpillar dozer and began the work of clearing land, constructing lakes, and ponds and digging foundations and basements for the postwar housing boom. All this effort, and the associated expectations of the community, took a toll on my father, so much so that he finally sold his interests in the construction effort to others and concentrated on the farm operation. During this early time, my uncle Henry also returned from World War II, became a Baptist minister, and also began a Dozer construction effort in Fountain Run, Kentucky. My uncle Fay Martin worked with my father, eventually taking over the dozer business and continuing to operate a long-distance family farm of his own.

I tried to always be my father's shadow, traveling with him where he would allow and riding on or in any vehicle or equipment that was permitted. On a trip in May 1959, I accompanied him to Grandpa's feed mill to grind a load of corn and hay for the dairy operation. Just before we turned into the barn at the top of the hill above the house, the brakes failed on the truck. My father thought he could get the truck 'geared down' and stopped, so he stayed on the road instead of 'crashing' the truck into the fence or ditch line. I can remember him trying to downshift the truck and it becoming caught between gears. He attempted to 'click' the 'hi-lo' range button to help with the neutral situation, to no avail. The transmission only growled and ground as he tried to get it in gear. During this time, it continued to gain speed down the hill. Dad finally reached for the emergency brake and gave it a mighty tug, only to have the drums on that system explode. At this point, we neared our home, and the road became steeper. I do not remember how fast we were travelling when we came to the bottom of the hill, but to an eight-year-old, it seemed very fast! We travelled about two hundred additional yards before we crossed a wooden culvert, immediately topping a short rise where our road made a ninety-degree transition to another road. There was a six-foot embankment just across the road. My dad made a huge effort to turn the truck, but momentum had taken over. I do not remember the crash. I do have recollections of people gathering around the truck cab and my father crying and pulling me from the truck. I remember arriving at our local community store and changing cars to the backseat of my grandfather's car. I somewhat remember the very fast ride from Three Forks to the Bowling Green Hospital, high on Hospital Hill. I seem to remember the sight of seeing that large brick structure through the windows of the car as we drove into the emergency room entrance.

My next recollection is of waking up on a very bright Sunday morning to my aunt Wanda being in the room. She was reading the cartoon section from the Sunday paper, and when I grunted, she jumped up and gathered the family into the room. I wondered why everyone was crying. I had been unconscious for some time after all the major surgery that was performed on my face. I have been given a fifty-fifty or less chance of survival. What had put me in this condition?

At the moment of impact of a two-ton truck, loaded with a weekly load of sacked feed and other things, hitting a six-foot red clay bank, inertia carried my eight-year-old frame from the seat into the dash of this Dodge truck. At that time, there were no plastic or vinyl amenities in farm trucks—only painted steel structure. The front of the truck deflected a little, the large wooden bed on the truck broke loose from the frame, sliding forward and pushed in the back of the truck cab like a compressed soda can. The load of feed on the truck was catapulted over the cab of the truck and landed twenty feet in our neighbor's field. A double-bitted axe that was secured in the bed of the truck went end over end and landed in one of the sacks of feed. The only spot that indicated a point of impact for me in the truck was the indentations where my open mouth had struck the metal dash. I understand there were distinctive upper and lower bite marks imbedded in the metal dash. When I woke up, I remember my dad climbing over the seat and pulling me out through the driver's side of the truck. Multiple surgeons worked many hours that day to save my life. My four upper front teeth and much of the maxilla were forced upward. These were removed from the nasal cavity, and the maxilla was reconstructed from all the broken bones and tissue. Removal of the four broken lower teeth and repair of that damage concluded a long surgical process. I am not sure what they felt their success would be, and I am sure they wondered what kind of brain damage or internal bleeding might occur later. After I woke up and responded to everyone normally and they determined there were no other problems, I remember Aunt Wanda reading each of the Sunday cartoons to me.

As an eight-year-old, I didn't really appreciate the future I would face regarding this incident. I had barely had my permanent teeth anyway, and I supposed a new set of permanent teeth would replace those lost. I was to learn this would never happen. I was to become a fourth-grader with partial dentures. My attitudes regarding the future did not improve with adolescence, and it sometimes seemed that parents and family thought the accident had made me more susceptible to breakage. Our distance from school, my injury, and farm activities limited my ability to participate in sports. It seemed to me a terrible time to become a man.

As the oldest, and apparently in an attempt to prove myself, I always tried to perform tasks on the farm two years earlier than normal. I was driving a tractor when I could only push the clutch and brake in by standing up and pulling on the bottom of the steering wheel. There was no power steering at that time on our tractors, so I had to get the tractor moving to turn it. Dad was always buying and selling cattle and would on some evenings be late coming home from the market. I always had the cows in the barn and the lights on when he arrived.

On one particular occasion, I determined to surprise him. We milked in a two-cow *V* parlor that was elevated about three feet. A pull cord on a weighted door allowed us to let two cows enter at a time. Our milker was a Surge system that required a strap over the cow's back and metal carrier to hang the milker. I felt I could begin the effort. I let the first two cows in to the parlor. I climbed the bars that defined the cow's stall and put the strap over the back of the cow. I climbed down and anxiously crawled under the cow to reach the metal hanger to hook into the strap. At his point, I had to use an old metal milk stool to stand on to get the stainless steel Surge milker on the floor where the cow was standing. I was not strong enough to raise it to reach the strap and hanger. I had to reach over the bar above the milker to gain enough leverage to jerk the milker up to the strap. I think I accomplished the task on the second try. Then I had to reach to the back of the milker and put the appropriate section on the appropriate udder. As I was being extra careful, the cow was a little nervous and moved some. I was afraid of being kicked during this effort. Luckily, the first cow into the parlor was a very patient cow. This cow was gentle and patient and also the herd's best producer. The milker was probably three-fourths full when the milking was completed. I had to jerk the milker off the strap and let if fall on the floor. I expected the cow to react in a bad way with all the noise. I grasped the milker with both hands and struggled across the *V* pit to the spot where we kept our cans. I had prepared the strainer, just as I had watched my dad do it. I was unable to pour the milk directly from the milker into the strainer, so I had to pour it into a milk bucket and then transfer it to the strainer. The milker was heavier than the bucket, so I had to put the bucket between the milk can and the milker to keep it from slipping away. I finally finished that first cow! I was so proud that I had gotten this done before my dad got home. Now, I only had about twenty more cows left to milk. I felt Dad would arrive at any time, but on this particular occasion, he was very late getting home. I finished the milking and struggled to get the cans into our eight-can spray cooler. I cleaned the parlor, fed the cows, turned out the lights, and walked down the hill in the dark autumn evening. I walked in to our evening meal and told Mom what I had done. She was upset for a while but was very proud of my initiative and effort. I do not remember what Dad said after getting home, but I do remember that more and more, it became an expectation that I could do the evening milking. This was to be the blueprint for my life, always having the confidence in what I could achieve and many times earning the opportunity to perform.

Not everyone will understand or laugh about what I have shared above. Those of you that grew up with or helped with the milking chores during this time will understand every element. I sometimes regret that I did not provide my children these opportunities to gain individual confidence. I have learned that there are always many different ways for youth to accomplish these same life lessons and that the most difficult part is our ability to relate life's lessons to each other from one generation to another.

During the 1960s, our nation was going through many structural and social upheavals. Our social topography became so much more diverse and relevant, becoming both variegated and leveled. During this time, the Dunn family moved back onto our farm to take over the milking responsibilities and assist with the other farming. Mr. Luther Dunn was my personal and very positive initiation to racial culture. My dad had decided to return to the dozer business, and this help was sorely needed. My brothers and I first met Mr. Luther Dunn when I was only eleven or twelve. He seemed a giant of a man, well over six feet and as broad as a door. His wife, Louise, was one of the kindest and caring ladies I have ever known. She always had a smile and kind word for the Smith youngsters. Their youngest son, Wayne Howard Dunn, was a year older than me. Their youngest daughter, Cathy, was about the same age as my sister.

Mr. Dunn chose not to develop the skills necessary to operate a tractor. He had driven a car a lot in earlier years but chose not to take the responsibility for tractors and implements. Mr. Dunn knew everything there was to know about draft animals, so my father purchased Mr. Dunn a team of mules, a like new John Deere team wagon, and all the implements necessary to cultivate gardens and tobacco. My brothers and I thoroughly enjoyed following Mr. Luther as he worked, talking to him and listening to his expressions regarding life. He would say, "I'm not fast, but I'm regular," laughing good-heartedly. He would indicate he was a "rambling piece of plunder" with a laugh and a melodic rhythm that we attempted to imitate. I was very much older when I finally realized the potential cultural implication of this message, but Mr. Luther Dunn always treated us as a gentlemanly mentor would. I know my brothers and I asked many inappropriate questions out of the pure inquiring minds of youth, and Mr. Dunn always answered these questions in a kind and considerate manner. I remember those days of life with fondness and much joy.

I accompanied Wayne Howard as we got the cows up to milk in the afternoons. We had two major ways to kill the time while getting the cows up. We would either be throwing rocks with the slings we fashioned from the tongues of old work shoes and baler twine or be hitting rocks with tobacco sticks we carried. I was always trying to outperform Wayne Howard in either of these, but I could never quite make it. He always had the same easy and comfortable laugh as his father. Our slings had a slip knot on one string and a hard knot tied in the free end. We always used a large shoe tongue, as we wanted to throw larger rocks. Our throws seemed to always be for distance, though we finally got good at knocking cans off fence posts. I guess we always wanted to be like David, as he slew Goliath!

Our exploits with tobacco sticks and rocks is another complete issue. Wayne Howard held the tobacco stick in his left hand, picked up the rock, and pitched it up in front of the stick before taking the swing. I observed and perfected the maneuver just as he performed it. I thought this was the only way to hit a rock. In later years, my children's coaches in softball and baseball were amazed to watch me hit the ball during practice like this. I never adopted any other way; I had learned from the best. There is one aspect of hitting small rocks with a tobacco stick; you develop excellent hand-eye coordination. The size of the rock doesn't matter as much in farm field hitting. You are concentrating on both the rock and getting all the power you can to it through the tobacco stick. The pleasure of all this effort is not in the distance you achieve, but in the acoustics of the effort. There is a very distinct *swish* that the stick makes when you swing it, a very solid *twack* that is both felt and heard, but the most pleasurable part of the experience is the *Z-I-N-n-n-g-g—g—g* that the rock makes from the time of impact throughout its flight. Once you are hooked on that sound, you begin looking for the angular rocks that will make the best sound. After hundreds of swings, you can hit any rock with almost no stick at all. I always felt this initial effort paved the way for me to hit baseballs and softballs without much effort. The bat and ball are so much larger than the stick and stone. There is artistry in performing this motion to accomplish the constant hits that just feels natural.

I did not take up golf in later years, but I understand that Wayne Howard became a natural golfer. I can envision that left hand grasping the club and powering the swing through that golf ball. I bet he is a distance golfer! I can only imagine the sound one of our stones had we had a Big Bertha to hit them.

When Mr. Dunn started milking, I was relieved of this twice daily task. After becoming large enough to really do the work, it became just that—work. No young person really appreciates work. While we helped with all the tasks on the farm, we never again got into milking. When Mr. Dunn and his family moved on to a better opportunity, we sold the cows and never milked again. One thing I promised myself at that time was that I would never do either of two things on any future farm: milk cows or raise hogs.

I appreciate the Dunn family more than they will ever know. I was more than confused and perplexed by the unrest we watched on television and read about in the papers during the times of unrest. I experienced none of this unrest or resentment while growing up, so it was unimaginable to me. I have come to understand that the violence of change does not come as much from circumstantial difference, but rather the inflamed rhetoric on either side of an issue. Too many people spend their lives and time trying to identify differences rather than working to achieve a common good.

I married my first love on June 28, 1969. LaDonna and I began our life together living with my grandparents. I continued my employment with Holley Carburetor in Bowling Green, foregoing my college after completing my first year at Western Kentucky University. During the next year, other friends married. Many friends were drafted for the Vietnam conflict, and we hosted a "lottery" party at our house to watch the dates drawn from the tumbler to determine the order of future draftee calls. Luckily, my number was very high. This was not so for my friend Steve Richey. He and his young wife left very disappointed that night. In June 1970, at the urging of my friend Doug Sturdivant, I joined the Kentucky National Guard as an enlisted teletype operator.

I joined the Guard just two days before my first wedding anniversary. I had not consulted LaDonna or family regarding this decision. It was one of those things that just seemed right to do at the time. June 26, 1970 changed my life forever, and I attribute my efforts with the 1st Battalion, 623rd Field Artillery as one of the most positive things I have ever done. I was selected in 1972 to become an Air Defense team chief. From this assignment and the recommendation of 1SG Billy Hall Baxter, I applied, was tested, was interviewed, and was selected to attend Officer Candidate School. In the intervening years, our first child, Angela Marie, was born. I was attending my intermediate radio school at Fort Knox, having just completed Basic Combat Training, when she was born. The staff charge of quarters (CQ) woke me up one cold February night to tell me I had a baby daughter. I jumped out of the bunk and started to gather my clothes. The CQ asked, "What are you doing?" I said I was ready for a pass to go be with them. He said, "Your wife and child are fine, and you don't get a pass to just go home." I went back to bed brokenhearted. Luckily, I was ready for the required Morse Code test. At that time, if you passed the test early, you got a three-day pass. When the test NCO heard my situation, I passed the test, got the three-day pass, and advanced to ship out to Fort Gordon, Georgia, after that. I got home in time to bring my family home from the hospital. It was a great feeling! The hard part was returning to Fort Knox, boarding a Greyhound bus, and driving right back down I-65 and past our home on the way to Fort Gordon.

My Officer Candidate School effort was as routine as any OCS experience anyone has ever experienced. OCS is not meant to be routine! Most classes lose 30 to 50 percent of the applicants. I was fortunate and completed the program in receipt of the Association of the United States Army Leadership Award for our class in June 1974.

Later that year, our second child, Leigh Ann, "Buffy," was born. Within a month of her birth, LaDonna and I loaded our family and reported to Fort Sill, Oklahoma, for Field Artillery Officer Basic Course training. Buffy rode on a pillow in the back seat of our car, guarded by her older sister Angela. This was my first major test of competence. My two other new Field Artillery Officers in the battalion and from my OCS class attended this same course. Upon arriving at Fort Sill, we were thrown in with West Point, ROTC, Marine, and other Guard officers to complete the training. Initial test outcomes placed me in a group with many West Pointers and veteran Marine officers. It was a great experience. I completed FAOBC on the Commandant's List. This trip to Fort Sill was enough for LaDonna. As our children got older and started school, she remained home with them throughout the remainder of my military training. Alison came along in 1976, and Patrick in 1984. I owe their excellent athletic abilities, their academic prowess, and their salvation to the efforts of their mother. She took them to practices, games, academic competitions, and meets throughout this period—most of the time while I was away for training, deployed, or working in a city too distant from home, allowing me to only spend most weekdays at home.

I was an honor graduate at the Field Artillery Survey Officer Course, and I was selected as a group leader at the Combined Arms and Services Staff School at Fort Leavenworth, Kansas. After becoming the full-time training officer for the 1st Battalion, 623rd Field

Artillery, I helped guide efforts that culminated in our battalion being named the Best Reserve Component Battalion in the 2nd United States Army area five times and being named as the Best Reserve Component Battalion in the United States twice. I was honored to be selected as the battalion commander and then to be called upon to deploy with these great men during Operation Desert Storm. I prayed to God to allow me to bring each of them home, and He blessed me with in this request.

After completing my battalion command tour of duty, I was transferred to Fort Knox to work with the Kentucky Military Academy coordinating and conducting training for National Guard and Reserve Non-Commissioned and Commissioned Officers. I was later selected as commandant of KMA. During this time, I helped as a regional representative of the National Guard Bureau as everyone in the Army transitioned to the Total Army School System. Due to efforts in this arena and my former battalion efforts, Major General John Groves selected me to serve as chief of staff of the Kentucky National Guard in Frankfort, Kentucky. I completed this duty and retired from military service in July 1998, having served twenty-eight years. During my final year, Major General Groves nominated me to fill a general officer position. The Chief of the National Guard Bureau concurred with this nomination and forwarded it to the Secretary of the Army. The nomination was declined at this level, due to the fact that I had not completed the United States Army War College, or its equivalent. This requirement had been in place during my last two years of service, and I felt that I could not dedicate the time away from my chief of staff responsibilities to attend a one-year course. Looking back, it seems God had other plans for me than becoming a general officer.

All these brief indications are to acquaint you with the life I led before becoming involved with Bluegrass ChalleNGe Academy in 2001. I grew up expecting to always do the right thing and expecting to work hard to achieve meaningful goals in life. God has always been there for me and has blessed every part of my life. There were times in my youth that I did not recognize this. Why did an accident have to happen that impacted every aspect of my development and participation? Was the early recognition of what might happen if I became intoxicated with my partial dentures the reason I chose not to drink with my peers? Did my father really drink enough for both of us when I was growing up? Why did God place me on a farm so far from school and town that attending practice became prohibitive? As I have grown older, and hopefully wiser, I recognize that God has used everything for my good. Our struggles are what make us strong and allow us to persevere in the face of hardships.

In July 1998, I retired from active military service as the chief of staff of the Kentucky Army National Guard. My service had included almost two years as chief of staff, a year as commandant of our state military academy and several years as the operations officer of the academy, command of the 1st Battalion, 623rd Field Artillery before and during deployment to Operation Desert Storm, and years of duties as operations officer, fire direction officer, battery commander, battery executive officer, forward observer, and enlisted service before Officer Candidate School. I tried always to lead by example and to demonstrate integrity with a steadfast vision to always choose the "more difficult right over the easier wrong." I fully believe my daily exhibition of these tenants were why Major General John R. Groves chose me as his chief of staff, over my protests that there were many more qualified colonels deserving of the position. Along the path of my military career, I was awarded the Legion of Merit twice, the Bronze Star medal, the Meritorious Service Medal multiple times, and many other awards. While serving as the operations officer of the 1st Battalion, 623rd Field Artillery, the battalion was recognized five times as the best Reserve Component Battalion in the Second United States Army area (Southeast United States) and twice recognized as the best Reserve Component Battalion in the United States! During my entire life, prior to this event, my only personal interaction with an attorney was with family members at family reunions or in regards to the purchase of property. I think I have received one speeding ticket in my life. I only share this background to establish my background as a military officer in the service of our country and a firm belief that one should follow the norms, rules, and expectations defined in the Bible and in our Constitution.

I have served in two local Baptist churches, teaching adult Sunday school classes in both, serving as a deacon in both, serving as moderator of business meetings in both, and serving on various committees in both. During the past year, I served on our Church Pastor Search Committee, being chosen by the other members as its chairperson.

Upon my retirement from the military, I returned to my family farm. Within a week of retirement, I was asked by an uncle to help him construct a new home. As he was a retired master carpenter, I was both excited and privileged by the opportunity to help him and learn from him. Nine months later, we had completed his construction, and my wife and I began the construction of our own dream home on our farm. This project lasted from March 1999 through May 2000. We sold one home (which we had personally constructed in 1978) and moved in our farm dream home on Derby Day 2000.

I spent the next year involved in community service and performing farm tasks relating to our Angus herd. This period also resulted in a very contentious presidential election, and I spent several hours watching the discussion of "chad" counting in Florida.

In mid-2001, I was contacted by Major General John Groves's former administrative assistant, Ms. Janet Newman, and asked to consider applying for a contract position with the Kentucky Youth ChalleNGe program. I was not inclined to apply, but upon investigation of the program and discussion with some old friends who worked there, I did apply. Colonel (Ret.) Joe Warren and I were selected for two positions and began duties as placement coordinators just after the attack on the World Trade Center in September 2001. I enjoyed my duties helping graduates of the Youth ChalleNGe program find jobs, enroll in college, join the military, or meet the expected placement criteria of the program. Joe and I came up with some innovative concepts and processes that were later considered and adopted by the National Guard Bureau and presented to the other Youth ChalleNGe programs for their consideration. Our efforts resulted in Kentucky Youth ChalleNGe, earning awards for Most Innovative Program and increasing our placement statistics to among the best in the nation. In 2003, I was asked to apply for the position of director of Bluegrass ChalleNGe Academy by other staff within the program and after the founding director had departed. On the last day of the opening, I reluctantly applied and was selected by a state board for the position. After the first nine months of duties as director, I realized I could not continue to manage the program and a family Angus herd. I sold my herd the following April and leased my farm to a church friend to grow row crops. This lease continues uninterrupted.

2

THE KENTUCKY YOUTH CHALLeNGe PROCESS

Every parent, when that child was first born, wanted him or her to be a success. Somewhere along the line something went wrong, but at (a Youth ChalleNGe) graduation all that past is made right.

—Joe Padilla

The National Guard Youth ChalleNGe program is the outcome of a need expressed by the Rockefeller Foundation Study in the late 1980s and Lieutenant General John B. Conaway, Chief, National Guard Bureau (and a Kentuckian) accepting the challenge when other Department of Defense agencies indicated it was not part of their war fighting mission.

The Rockefeller Foundation Study reflected the growing national risk related to an ever-increasing level of high school dropouts. Unless corrected, these trends predicted a time when the United States would be unable to meet the required technical skills for industry, government, or the military. Something must be done to address the growing at-risk youth epidemic. The study participants searched for periods and mechanisms that prepared our youth for service in times of much need, times where our national outcome depended upon and delivered these results. It became readily apparent that no other organizational model in America's history had been more efficient and more effective in producing leaders capable of responding to both technical and life-and-death situations than the basic training model developed for each of our military services during World War II. This model trained and developed college graduates, factory workers, small-town athletes, farm boys, and small business workers for the stresses and needs of combat. The model developed in the 1930s remains in use today.

While the study participants recognized there was no need for any martial training in a program for at-risk youth, they did recognize that the structural aspects of the basic training company cohort seemed to provide a perfect model for program development. Much of the training model was evaluated, and it was modified to produce the desired change in lives of youth who were capable yet disenfranchised, youth who had been in trouble but no serious trouble, and youth who had made mistakes but desired change in their lives.

Seven core components and several key enrollment outcomes were developed. To attend, youth must be:

- sixteen to eighteen years of age at the time of entry into the program
- A high school dropout
- A citizen or legal resident of the United States
- Unemployed or underemployed
- Not convicted of a felony or currently on parole or probation
- Free from use of illegal drugs or substances
- Physically and mentally capable to participate in the program

The seven core components of the program proposal included:

- Academic Excellence
- Health and Hygiene
- Job Skills
- Leadership/Followership
- Life Coping Skills
- Physical Fitness
- Responsible Citizenship

Readily recognized is the connection with the non-martial aspects of military basic training and the outcomes expected by the study participants. The study manager, having seized upon the basic training model as the primary structural component, visited the primary Department of Defense elements to obtain service buy in. None of the primary services, at this time of mission reduction and cuts, indicated any desire to participate. As a last-chance gesture, the proposal was presented to Lieutenant General Conaway. General Conaway recognized the need and the potential for the National Guard to become the lead element in the effort. The National Guard was America's military team, with armories in most counties or parishes throughout the country. The National Guard is composed of former members of all services and many involved local business leaders, workers, educators, and church members. The opportunity for federal-state cooperative funding agreements existed within the organizational fiscal model of the National Guard. All these wide spread and different points of contact within communities assured that the identification of potential at-risk students, and local mentors to support their first year after graduation would be easily identified. Lieutenant General John B. Conaway paved the way for a very successful national program on that day.

The combined efforts of the National Guard and the Rockefeller Foundation resulted in Congress implementing, in the early 1990s, pilot performance studies and evaluations. These studies rapidly produced and exceeded the expected Rockefeller Foundation predictions. Congress created the permanent legal authorization for the National Guard Youth ChalleNGe program under Title 32 United States Code (USC) § 509. Kentucky joined the National Guard

Youth ChalleNGe family under the Executive Order of Governor Paul Patton in 1998. Two buildings on Fort Knox, formerly occupied by Kentucky Military Academy, were selected as the operational site for Bluegrass ChalleNGe Academy. Colonel (Retired) Elmo "Rock" Head was identified as the first director. An expedited effort to select, train, and equip the program resulted in the first class beginning in July 1999. Colonel Head and Ms. Janet Newman worked to insure the Kentucky program wasted no time in catching up to the earlier programs and developed new processes and techniques to improve Youth ChalleNGe. Governor Patton appointed members of several important cabinets within state government as a steering committee to insure the success of Youth ChalleNGe.

As the program grew, Colonel Head recognized the need to expand the staffing to insure there was dedicated effort toward the placement of BCA graduates in education, jobs, or the military. He and Ms Newman secured a grant to hire two contract positions to implement the grant objectives and develop processes for the future. As Ms Newman had been Major General Groves's administrative assistant when he was the adjutant general and our duties required day-to-day interactions, she called to advise me of the need and opportunity. I was enjoying my retirement but applied due to her expressed confidence and the need. Colonel Joe Warren and I were selected for the positions. We hit the ground running. Joe took all of Kentucky East of I-65, and I took Louisville and all of Kentucky West of I-65. We both participated in training activities at Fort Knox, but our primary responsibilities were to insure placement and contact reporting by mentors. Kentucky made some major strides in this area due to that grant.

Colonel Head left Bluegrass ChalleNGe Academy in early 2003. Everyone lamented his departure, and no one seemed to be ready to step forward to apply for the position. Nearing the end of the application period, Colonel (Ret.) Tom Rickerd called me to urge me to apply. He indicated, "Are you going to apply, or am I going to fill out the application for you?" After considering this urging, I did complete the application. Major General Allen Youngman, the adjutant general at the time, asked that a statewide board be conducted, even though this process is not generally conducted for a non-merit division director within Kentucky. I interviewed in Frankfort and was selected. On the day we visited Governor Patton, as he was required to sign the appointment, he became confused when Major General Youngman indicated I was the unanimous board selection. Governor Patton was confused as he had never been required to sign the appointment of a director chosen by board action.

As I assumed the director's position, I was advised that the program had experienced some very serious problems with staff and cadet interactions, resulting in less-than-flattering media for our effort. My charge was to continue the record of accomplishment I had demonstrated in my past assignments and put my tenets of character-based management in place to correct these problems. This would have been my only plan of action, had I not been instructed in this manner! While there were some issues between 2003 and 2013; my consistent efforts with Fort Knox leadership, the Provost Marshall, CID, the Hardin County Sheriff's office, and the legal advisor of the Department of Military Affairs for the Kentucky National Guard resulted in no staff or cadre being charged with any crimes. I did lose staff and cadre for various reasons during the period, some of which included issues I proposed charges be filed with the provost marshal or state agencies. Responses in each case were that the incidents were not chargeable offenses. I was advised to instruct families they could pursue civil actions if they desired.

I learned very quickly that the director's job was closer to that of the chief of staff than I had imagined. I not only coordinated the activities of the division with Frankfort but the National Guard Bureau also made the director the state point of contact regarding all Youth ChalleNGe issues. This was not the normal process, as the normal chain of responsibility between National Guard Bureau is the chief to the adjutant general of the states, commonwealths, and territories. In any organization, if the higher staff element can bypass the intermediate headquarters and obtain action at the staff element of responsibility, it will occur. All the complaints, threats, and action requirements from NGB came directly to me. Most of the positive information went through the chief, NGB to the adjutant general.

The many Youth ChalleNGe directors around the nation all operate in a slightly different organizational environment. Each state, commonwealth, or territory operates in a slightly different fashion. Each state has distinct rules and procedures regarding how personnel are hired, how they are paid, how they are trained, and how any equipment and materials are procured. Each has different processes regarding service contracting and execution. Youth ChalleNGe is a state-run organization, with federal matching funds flowing from the congressional budget through the Department of Defense to National Guard Bureau. National Guard Bureau executes a federal-state Master Youth Programs Cooperative Agreement for the operation of the program. The rules and requirements for the operation of the program are spelled out in this agreement. Any failure to meet the contractual agreements can result in the cancellation of the contract or the potential identification of processes completed that are not in accordance with contract guidelines, resulting in the requirement for the state to reimburse the federal government their 75 percent of that expenditure action. Each state, commonwealth, or territory already executes many other cooperative agreements through the United States Property and Fiscal Officer (USPFO) in their geographic area. The USPFO monitors all state expenditures and contracts to insure that all fiscal law requirements are appropriately executed. They perform periodic audits of program operations and accounts. They provide oversight on all annual expenditures, above and beyond the state's fiscal management efforts.

Each program in the nation operates with ample operational oversight. Bluegrass ChalleNGe Academy was under the direct supervision of the executive director, Office of Management and Administration, Department of Military Affairs. The adjutant general, appointed by the governor, was the final supervisory authority. Operational supervision included various elements within the department that included personnel, purchasing, contracting, payroll, facilities maintenance, information management, and others. We received all program operational directions from National Guard Bureau. They modified the national Master Youth Program Cooperative Agreement from time to time and expected immediate modification to whatever areas the changes impacted. There were very strict limits on the numbers of positions that could be filled, what those positions were, what equipment could and could not be purchased, and what administrative processes and reporting must occur. As we occupied facilities on Fort Knox, there were rules and processes we were required to follow there as well. Most involved the safety requirements for the cadets as they trained on Fort Knox facilities or on Fort Knox roads. We paid our utility costs to Fort Knox. We had to gain approval from Fort Knox for any improvements or maintenance we performed on the facilities. We requested support through the same processes as units assigned to the post. As I had served as the commandant of the Kentucky Military Academy just before becoming chief of staff and had only been retired for three years, many of the key civilian personnel were in key positions when I returned as director. Mr. Emmet Holley, as the civilian deputy garrison commander, was an asset I depended upon constantly. Mr. Bill Hickock was the Fort Knox Facilities director who had helped me relocate the Kentucky Military Academy from World War II–era buildings to the modern buildings across post. These were the same buildings I returned to when I became director. My old commandant's office was occupied by the academy teachers when I returned, and I enjoyed telling them that on occasion.

As you can readily see, there were many opportunities for multiple agencies to tell us how to accomplish our jobs. If it were a task that we felt NGB should complete, they might reply, "You belong to a state program, and the federal government has no responsibility to meet this need." If I went to Fort Knox for law enforcement assistance, they often told us that we were a state program and unless our cadets were military dependants, we should contact the Hardin County Sheriff's office or the Kentucky State Police. If we called the Hardin County Sheriff's office or the Kentucky State Police, they would say that they have no jurisdiction on Fort Knox and that we should call the military police. There seemed always to be an apparent expression by everyone that someone else was the appropriate resource.

The hot potato process did not happen in all instances at Fort Knox. We generally received excellent support from post regarding facilities, utilities, maintenance, training area utilization, training approvals, and medical operations. I tried to decentralize these efforts to the appropriate office within the academy, and they made everything work as it should. We used cycle breaks to accomplish routine training requirements from NGB, Kentucky, and Fort Knox and to provide staff some needed vacation time, where accumulated compensatory time was used. I will state here and later too, that at no time during my service to BCA did anyone ever provide a briefing regarding the responsibilities of 42 USC § 13031, identify any "designated agency," provide any "reporting format," or conduct any initial or periodic training regarding this statute. When I say anyone, I include the Kentucky Department of Military Affairs, National Guard Bureau and any of their contracted trainers, any agency so designated by Fort Knox, the provost marshal, the military police commander, the Criminal Investigation Detachment (CID) commander, or the judge advocate general corps officer representing the attorney general on Fort Knox.

My tenure as director lasted 10.5 years. This was 5.5 years longer than I initially anticipated, but working to help cadets graduate and go on to achieve goals they had come to believe were outside their reach made the 1.5-hour daily, one-way drive acceptable. With the help of supportive adjutant generals and Department of Military Affairs executive directors, we were able to change Kentucky Youth ChalleNGe in many meaningful ways. We added a high school credit recovery dimension to what had been a strictly GED educational element. We exceeded our graduation target for the first time and accomplished that in four other classes while I was at Fort Knox. We worked to expand Kentucky Youth ChalleNGe into the Appalachian region and were able to help the Appalachian ChalleNGe Academy open its doors in Harlan County, Kentucky. To date, and since my retirement, ACA is the only Kentucky Youth ChalleNGe academy to repeat my target gradation accomplishment. During my tenure as director, over 1,820 youth graduated from Bluegrass ChalleNGe Academy, and another two hundred graduated from Appalachian

ChalleNGe Academy before I retired. I remain very proud of the achievements of the academies, the cadet graduates, and the staff members who work many long and difficult hours toward the mental and physical rebirth of our cadets.

I was very naïve during my first year as director. I had the impression that my demonstrated care and compassion for the cadets would be the reason that each of them would be successful. I felt this extra care and compassion would be emulated by all staff and cadre, resulting in the dramatic increase in our performance, both in numbers and in postgraduate accomplishment. I departed home at 4:30 a.m. Central Time each day and started work at 7:00 a.m. Eastern Time (crossing the time zone occurred twice each day). My early days were spent examining the existing processes and procedures. I had commanded the Kentucky Military Academy and understood the processes and procedures for both officer candidate and noncommissioned officer training. I had worked during that time as one of the regional representatives of National Guard Bureau in implementing the Army's Total Army School System (TASS) within the Reserve Components. I found that BCA policy and procedures were well defined and executed very aptly.

Part of the national Youth ChalleNGe process is to both create stress within the first two weeks but also provide instruction and support during the time. Days begin early with personal hygiene, formations, raising the flag, physical training, showers, breakfast, basic instruction on formations, leadership, marching, sexual harassment, policy and procedures (the Blue Book), issue of clothing, expectations of uniformity, teaching the cadets what must be maintained in their personal area, and their collective areas. We taught them lawn mower safety because at that time we used push mowers and the cadets mowed the grass. We taught members of each platoon how to clean and buff the platoon floors. I expected a hospital floor shine on each floor. Our young ladies had some extra duties regarding the floors in the headquarters building as they were the sole cadet occupants of that building. I personally showed two volunteers how to care for the floors each cycle. I always thanked them for the excellent work they did. I always informed the commandant and the male platoon sergeants that the ladies were doing a much better job of maintaining their building than our male cadets were. This only made the ladies more diligent in their efforts.

In every cycle, we had many cadets who felt unable to continue the program after the fourth or fifth day. Myriad examples of excuses were concocted and shared by cadet candidates. We witnessed cadet candidates throw tantrums or go into complete shutdown, refusing to comply with any instructions. Part of the program effort was to demonstrate to the youth that we fully expected self-sufficiency on their part. This was not a program to try for a few days and then depart if it did not "feel good." In later cycles, I shared in my initial briefings to cadets and parents alike, stating, "Cadets cry for four of the twenty-two weeks they participate in the program. They cry during the first two weeks because they don't want to be here, and they cry for the last two weeks because they don't want to leave." The goal of the entire staff was to get cadets past those first two or three weeks. On every occasion during my first cycles, disenchanted cadet candidates (they became full-fledged cadets after hard-core graduation at the end of the first two weeks) were required to share their concerns with the cadre, then the platoon supervisor, then the performance counselor, then the commandant, and then the director. This process elevated the cadets concerns to a higher level each time and in the process allowed the program to address the concerns of the cadet at the lowest level possible. Sometimes this worked for cadets who were not fully invested in their desires to "quit." I tried to delay seeing cadets until late in the day, and if we felt the cadet required a parental visit, we called the parents to come to the academy. Many such visits occurred. These necessary visits insured I did not get home until after 7:00 p.m. (Central Time) on many occasions.

By the time a parent or family was called to visit, the cadet had gone through a lot of time talking to someone and being encouraged. If they got to my office and knew their parents were coming, then they felt they were homeward bound, back to the refrigerator, the TV and remote, the cell phone, and the ability to roam the streets at all hours of the night with their friends. I scheduled most visits at night, as most parents worked day jobs. It was a simple equation for me. My staff had been gaining experience for four years and under-stood the process better than I did. After my third parent conference, I learned the ins and outs of the visit. By the middle of week 1, my parent conferences took on a new agenda. I talked to the parents, and whoever had come with them, prior to bringing in the child. I explained the steps I would take during the actual conference and that the conference would proceed somewhat like this. I will bring in the cadet and ask them some general questions about their last twen-ty-four hours. I will ask what training had they participated in, what they had for breakfast, what they had for lunch, and what they had for their previous evening meal. Most cadets wanted to leave many of the offered items out of their recounting, so I would use the menu and fill in the blanks. Invariably, the cadet would indicate that this was available, but they didn't want any of that. Most parents were amazed to hear the selections the cadets had during the day. I then told the parents that I would ask the cadet, "Why do you want to go home?" I indicated, "Your child will tell you that they have enjoyed their time at BCA but that they have learned their lesson and would never disrespect them or disobey them again." I advised the parents to share with their child that they could see the difference in their child already and that they felt he or she should give the process another week or so in order to get over the apparent homesickness. I explained that their child would then move into phase 2 of their effort to go home. They would state something to the effect that "you wouldn't treat Billy or Jane this way. Why are you punishing me more than you would them?" I advised them to continue to resist and explain that what they have seen or heard indicates the program is very good and exactly what the recruiter said it would be. He indi-cated the first two or three weeks were the most difficult and your father and I want you to be more of an adult and continue for two or three weeks. If you don't change your mind by first pass, you can stay home then. I then explained that the cadet would immediately go to phase 3, that final effort to break the heart of the mother and go home. They would say, "If you don't take me home tonight, I will never speak to you again! I don't *love you*, since you apparently *don't love me!*" I shared that some parents don't make it through this final effort but to remain strong and continue their conviction and trust in our efforts. I shared that at this point, if you are confident in the child remaining, you should tell the child you will always love them but that they need to learn how to act like an adult. Tell them you will write and wait for their calls and that you are leaving. Get up, hug them, and leave. At this point, the parents were prepared.

I then called for the cadet to be brought to my office or the conference room for the meeting. The cadet came in smiling and bouncing in the expectation that all would be as they desired. I had the cadet take a seat and assume the proper posture of respect. I then began my process, and it always went exactly as I stated. In many instances, the parents responded as I asked, and the cadet remained and graduated. On one memorable instance, the male cadet grabbed his mother's purse and arm and tried to hold on to her as she was leaving. She pulled his hand off her arm and told him she loved him and departed. He cried then stubbornly indicated he would do nothing else. I allowed him to sit there for a few minutes then told him, "If you are going to continue to do nothing, you can do it somewhere else, as I must work in my office." We moved him to the outside steps on the building and made sure he had a canteen full of water. About thirty minutes later, he noticed the other cadet candidates having fun performing one of the training tasks, and he joined them. He never complained again and became one of the honor graduates for that class.

On occasions where my warnings or the parents' resolve weren't equal to the task at hand and the mother relented to the cadet candidate's desire to go home, I called the cadre on duty in to pick up the youth, get his or her personal clothing, and collect the academy items so we could sign them out. In every instance, the parent would ask, "How did you know what they would say and when they would say it?" On several occasions, the cadet would tell some crazy story regarding something that had happened. If the parent wanted them to go home, after they were ready for me to sign them out, I confronted their story in front of their parents. I indicated, "Your papers are signed, and you are going home. This is no trick, so would you tell your parents the truth in my presence regarding your earlier statement?" The cadet would smile and tell me and his parents that his or her statement was just a lie to get the parents to take him home.

I must tell one final story regarding a very intelligent young lady who attended BCA. Her parents were both licensed professionals from their town. We had made it through one parent conference in the first week of the program, and the young lady tried to get past the homesickness. Her disposition and attitude changed in the second week, and we had to call her parents back for a second visit. As the young lady had figured out my process after the first meeting, she somewhat repeated it. The father and mother tried everything they could to convince the young lady to stay. It was evident that the family had attempted these heartfelt and logical discussions in the past. During one point in the discussion, the mother shared that she had received the daughter's letter and had gone to her room to read it. She was so happy with the child's expressed confidence in her ability that as she sat on her bed and read the letter, she had cried deeply. The entire effort in my office changed at that moment. The young lady was more determined than ever to go home. After much discussion and time, the parents gave in and took her home. When she came back to my office, after changing and ready to go home, I shared with her and her mother, "When your mother told you that she sat on your bed, read your letter, and cried, you knew you had her, didn't you"? The young lady only looked at me and smiled.

After the encounters of the first two cycles and my getting home around 9:00 p.m. Central time, only to get up and go again at 4:30, I began to understand the experience and competence of my staff. I learned that they were as compassionate and caring as I was and that their efforts were as successful as mine. When everyone understood what I intended both cadets and parents to understand before any child went home, I allowed my commandant and the platoon sergeants to do their jobs. At some point, the commandant only brought cadets to my office that he felt might respond to me personally. This seemed to have a better outcome than my initial requirements. It is much better to have someone in the chain of command evaluate and only elevate those cases to the top that may respond to that consideration. I always had a great commandant.

During my ninth year as director, I could see that it would soon be time to transition to full retirement. I began discussing the potential of my future retirement with Colonel (Ret.) Mike Jones, the executive director of the Department of Military Affairs, and attempted to chart a smooth transition process. BCA was doing great and hitting graduate numbers above our targets routinely, and ACA was moving forward. My travel distance was not getting any shorter, and the 180 miles each day that I travelled had worn out multiple cars. We discussed personnel and an acceptable opportunity to retire, constantly looking for opportunities to prepare the way for future transition.

In early March 2013, Major General Tonini initiated a change to place all Youth ChalleNGe admissions efforts under the control of the federal civil service Kentucky National Guard recruiting manager. I had attempted to gain referrals from the National Guard recruiters without any positive result and felt this new effort would diminish the impact of our well-developed admissions, mentoring, and placement regional process. I took this change and my inability to have any input in the implemented change as the final indication that Frankfort was taking my intention to retire quite seriously. I therefore submitted a letter to General Tonini, indicating that I desired to execute my retirement in July 2013. General Tonini responded by asking that I consider staying on additional months, as he felt three months was an insufficient amount of time to identify a suitable replacement. I initially asked to perform my duties as a "part-time" director but was advised that there was no provision in state personnel procedures for a part-time director. I consented to remain through December 2013, with the understanding that I would remain on my four-day, ten-hour day schedule and would expect to also use up much of my accrued leave by taking additional Mondays off when practical. During this entire transition period, I immediately responded to all calls and messages from staff at Fort Knox, Harlan, Frankfort, and Washington whether I was at Fort Knox or home.

During this time, I was blessed by having a very experienced staff in all academy management areas. My transition could have occurred at any time with my deputy, SGM (Ret.) Gordon Disch assuming the role as director, either temporarily until a new director was selected or even with him being selected as the director. SGM (Ret.) Disch had worked at the program longer that me, and his service as both a former drill instructor and a US Army military police veteran made him an indispensable member of the team. One thing every military leader hopes to accomplish is to prepare a well-trained and dedicated staff to support their successor. Unfortunately, in military units, the concurrent rotation and reassignment of staff coincides with the leader's departure, precluding this ability. In Youth ChalleNGe, providing a well-trained and dedicated staff is much easier. Before one prepares to step aside and watch the organization march on, the leader must establish a very pure mission focus within every element of the organization. I felt I had accomplished this at BCA. Each of the many parts knew exactly what their actions did to compliment the total effort. It was much easier to allow the organization to function, watching the processes in place function, based not on my personal approval but for the good of the cadets and the organization. I remained concerned that major organizational structure changes, moving key responsibilities to elements not even connected with Youth ChalleNGe, would diminish the overall cohesion we had accomplished. Unfortunately, time proved these concerns to be justified.

Key BCA staff members, involved in the situation expressed in this story include:

1SG Leroy Burgess served as the Commandant of Bluegrass ChalleNGe Academy during much of my tenure as director. I was fortunate to know three great commandants during my time at BCA. Mr. Bryce Shumate was the commandant under Colonel (Ret.) Elmo Head while I was a placement coordinator. Bryce had a background in law enforcement and is married to District Judge Kimberly Shumate. Bryce grew up on Fort Knox and was very familiar with the workings of the post. He ran Cadet Operations with a firm and fair hand. Bryce accepted a position with the Radcliff Police Department about the time I came on board as director. Ms. Edna Seabrooks was another exceptional commandant during a short period in the middle of my director career. Ms. Seabrooks's background as a senior NCO in the US Army Reserve and a licensed counselor gave her great depth of understanding in the problems felt by the cadets and the staff as well as the military structure we utilized as the behavioral change agent. Ms. Seabrooks left Youth ChalleNGe after approximately eighteen months to accept a leadership role managing youth detention centers for the Commonwealth of Kentucky. After Shumate and Seabrooks; 1SG Burgess was the rock I depended on to manage the "Corps of Cadets" and their activities. His background as a US Army infantry-man and growing up in a rural setting in South Carolina provided much common ground for our relationship. 1SG Burgess also had counseling background in previous jobs after his military retirement. 1SG Burgess understood exactly what I expected regarding both staff and cadet performance, executing his duties in such a manner as I never had reason to doubt his actions.

Ms. Kemmye Graves was one of the initial employees when Bluegrass ChalleNGe Academy was formed in early July 1999. Kemmye was hired as an instructor and worked to prepare students for success with their GED testing. Kemmye was asked early on by Colonel (Ret.) Head to become one of his Equal Employment Opportunity Commission (EEOC) representatives. She and Mr. Dennis Elsey shared these duties when I was hired as a placement coordinator and continued after I became director. Mr. Elsey later succumbed to cancer, but not before becoming a valiant example to staff and cadets alike. When I asked Ms. Graves if she needed another EEOC representative to help, she declined indicating that she could handle the duties and those of her current position, academy policy and budget analyst. Ms. Graves developed many of the perennial events of the Academy. She initiated a Black History Month play during the February cycles. She organized a cadet talent show for each class. Kemmye and Nurse Cissell organized an Academy Easter Egg hunt for the spring classes. Many of our youth had never experienced an Easter Egg hunt. Kemmye is very involved in her church and also was a very respected foster parent, working with the Elizabethtown, Kentucky Department of Community Based Services to help with emergency placements of children, to include infants. Kemmye routinely discussed difficult EEOC investigations with the other EEOC staff in Frankfort and even at DCBS staff in Elizabethtown. Her goal was to always do the correct thing to resolve issues she investigated. While these discussions with DCBS were always valuable to her, there was seldom a record of the call or discussion. I always expected, and received, a very accurate and honest report regarding Kemmye's efforts; whether in policy, budget, or EEOC efforts.

MSG Gabriel Onusko was a gentleman I met very late in my tenure as director. He was recommended by a serving cadre who indicated "SGT O" was his drill sergeant in basic training and that he had become a mentor to him. This recommendation from an exceptional young cadre was about all it took for me to want to understand SGT O better. I was happy to forward the recommendation of the hiring board to Frankfort, with my endorsement regarding his selection. He served up to the measure his mentee had described as a cadre and was selected during a board action to move up to a platoon sergeant supervisor role. I always found MSG Onusko to be true, honest, and understanding of his role. I later found that this gentleman had grown up, served in, and retired from the US Army and worked in other roles before Youth ChalleNGe and had *never* been involved with any criminal charge—not even a speeding ticket—throughout his life.

PSG Rolanshia Windom was a female cadre who learned the role of cadre having never served in the military, other than as a spouse of someone who had served. Her very important gift was her empathy with the cadets, her willingness to listen to their problems and troubles, and her ability to suggest outcomes while maintaining the level of professionalism required. Ms. Windom struggled with personal health issues during my last year at BCA but never let these problems detract from her ability to serve the cadets.

PSG Rita Carthen was another female cadre with service in the US Army. Ms. Carthen was a longtime veteran of BCA and also had worked a second job with the day care at the church she attended. I was never completely clear as to why Ms. Carthen's name was ever considered in this case, as she was not even on shift at the time the later allegation regarding Jane Doe #1 occurred.

I will not share my personal evaluation of Stephen Miller, the supervisor who became the center of the problems we all experienced, other than to state that he was an exemplary cadre and supervisor up until the time I asked that the CID investigate an allegation by a female cadet in August 2013. He had served as a US Marine military police, served as a police officer in Leitchfield, Kentucky, served as a cadre in the male platoons for a couple of years, left the program voluntarily to pursue management opportunities in his hometown to be with his children for sports (as his shifts at BCA sometimes prevented this), and later asked to return to BCA as a cadre with the male cadets. He was often named by the male cadets as that "staff or cadre having the most positive impact" during their stay at the academy. He was selected, along with three other cadre, to assume the role of shift supervisor in late 2012. As we had selected four individuals that day, I gave the order of selection of a desired platoon to each person, based upon their place on the board selection. The first two took assistant platoon sergeant positions in the male platoons. SGT Onusko declined the platoon sergeant position in the First Platoon (female), stating that he would rather work for the final selectee. That is how this particular supervisor selection process fell into place.

There are a large number of other staff members that were important to both the program and to me as director. Nurse Tania Cissell and her nursing staff generally heard every story and allegation that occurred within the program. Due to Ms. Cissell's willingness to share issues of concern with me, many staff and cadre shared things with her as a means of getting the word to me, as many former military staff are reluctant to "go to the colonel." That Nurse Cissell and Ms. Graves were best of friends, having both begun their BCA efforts in the same office, helped with the sharing of important information. Ms Vicky Newton, Ms Andrea Percell, Mr. Jerry Glass, MSG Delbert Richardson, MSG Glenn Campbell, PSG Michael Shepherd, Mr. Troy Hampton and a wonderful team of teachers, and Mr. Mike Major were indispensible members of our management team.

As I prepared to depart BCA and Kentucky Youth ChalleNGe, I felt very confident that the organization was equipped to continue and prosper in my future absence and that the fundamental tenants of the program would be preserved. The routine nature of the organization changed on the morning of Friday, August 9, 2013, when I received an early e-mail reporting an allegation by one of our female cadets that she had been forced to have sexual contact with one of the male supervisors. While Friday was my regular day off, I remained in contact with my staff on all days away from the academy by phone or e-mail. I immediately advised my commandant, 1SG Roy Burgess, to contact the Fort Knox Criminal Investigation Detachment (CID) to investigate the incident. 1SG Burgess indicated he had asked Ms. Kemmye Graves to conduct an initial investigation but that she had not responded to him (Ms. Graves was at the time on the way to Western Kentucky to perform Department of Military Affairs duties as the third party in a state personnel hiring board and was unavailable to investigate anything). I directed 1SG Burgess to contact the CID immediately as the nature of the allegation required immediate involvement of an agency outside Bluegrass ChalleNGe Academy. 1SG Burgess contacted the CID, and they took charge of the investigation within the hour after my being notified.

I remained in close contact with the CID, and later the FBI, as they investigated the allegation. I provided copies of all requested materials and conducted interviews with the CID to fill in the blanks on their investigations. My entire staff stepped up to support the investigation. The CID representative, Special Agent Kyle Buckout, notified me in November 2013 that their involvement in the investigation had ended as the respondent in the case was not an active military member and the claimant was not the dependant of a military member. CID informed me that FBI special agent Mark Coleman would take over as the investigation lead. As of 31 December 2013, my retirement date, the investigation was still open, and I notified the FBI that my successor would be taking over responses for any academy material that was required. I departed Kentucky Youth ChalleNGe in December 2013. I was concerned that such an allegation had been made in August and still not sure why there was no closure in December.

3

THE CAMPAIGN PROCESS

I don't know what your destiny will be, but one
thing I know, the only ones among you who will
be happy are those who have sought and found
how to serve.

—Albert Schweitzer

The only thing necessary for the triumph of evil
is for good men to do nothing.

—Edmund Burke

In November 2013, I filed as a Democratic candidate for state representative in Kentucky's newly redistricted Nineteenth House District. I had decided that my ability to serve was not finished, that my contacts with Kentucky legislators on the state and national level while in the military and as director of Kentucky Youth ChalleNGe would provide the opportunity to make a difference in the lives of the citizens in the Nineteenth District. The year 2014 began with a new mission and new tasks to perform.

I campaigned as a Democrat. My grandfather Smith was a Democrat, my father was a Democrat, and most of my fraternal families were Democrats. My mother was a Republican, and her mother's family members (Humphreys) were charter members of the Republican party from Iowa. I grew up living my mother's conservative views and my father's family's beliefs that the Democratic party served to protect the common man. My personal political views were hybridized along these lines from an early age.

During my military career, I followed military tradition by remaining neutral regarding political issues. This is the expectation for military officers and an expectation that has served our country well. At no time should a person exerting influence over the lives of young men and women try to exert their personal political views on them. A leader's subordinates must have confidence that the person leading them has the mission and their individual well-being as their only goal.

I had completed a very blessed and successful military career. I was completing a very successful effort with Kentucky Youth ChalleNGe, having moved Bluegrass ChalleNGe Academy from minimal performance to among the best outcomes in the national efforts. I had helped establish Appalachian ChalleNGe Academy, causing Kentucky to join California, Georgia, and Louisiana as a state with multiple locations. I had served as a regional legislative liaison for the national Youth ChalleNGe effort. I had worked with legislators, legislative staff personnel, and constitutional agencies at both the national and state level. Our efforts had improved the outcomes of Youth ChalleNGe and previously the Kentucky National Guard. I knew the processes and many of the people involved. I was, and remain, confident of my ability to recognize ways to improve processes that impact people's lives. This reasoning, coupled with the recent legislative redistricting in Kentucky, affirmed my faith that I could continue to make a positive difference.

I ended 2013 by expressing my intentions to campaign for the Kentucky House of Representatives seat in the newly redistricted Nineteenth House District. I shared this information with key friends and family, with the Democratic executive committees in the two counties covered by District 19. I contacted my cousin, former Representative Roger Thomas, for support and advice. While Roger was serving our Commonwealth in a very demanding position as the chairperson of the governor's Council on Agriculture Policy, and he later also became the governor's legislative liaison, he always took time to comment and advise during my campaign. I also received valuable advice from our long time magistrate Tommy Hunt and received support from both executive committees and my fellow candidates for office. I found the camaraderie of candidates, whether those seeking Democratic office or the nonpartisan candidates to be among the most personally rewarding experiences of my life.

The early efforts of the campaign involved attending many Democrat party gatherings, obtaining the experiential advice of former candidates, obtaining the lists of voters in previous elections, and conducting private evaluations of previous elections to determine the impacts of presidential races, gubernatorial races, and local impacts of special campaigns. At that time, I felt I could predict the nature of issues important to the electorate in District 19. As in public speaking, the successful candidate must know their audience and be considered a part of that audience. I had grown up in and thought I knew each part of District 19. What I did not realize was how much parts of this area had changed in those seemingly short years while I had been serving state and country.

It was impressed upon me very early in my campaign that fund-raising was paramount to conducting an effective effort. I was urged to consider hiring a campaign manager and that I should focus much of my effort on asking people for money. This was foreign to my background, and I resisted it as much as possible. While the campaign raised, and spent, many thousands of dollars, I attribute 50 percent of my fund-raising effort to Roger Thomas and his knowledge of the process. Roger and his lovely wife, Doris, hosted a fundraiser for me that garnered the largest share of my funds. I was able to utilize public records to identify organizations that shared fundamental goals of our party and wrote each of them early on. Almost all these organizations responded with some support of our campaign. This is the only effort where I felt my personal involvement resulted in significant fund-raising. I felt I had the required funding to mount a successful campaign.

Very early in the process I dedicated my year to meeting the voters of Northern Warren and Edmonson counties. I wanted to catch up on the needs and the problems associated with government actions in the district. I attended as many of the county fiscal court meetings as I could in both counties, as I felt this is the closest element of government affecting the people in the district. I listened to many fiscal and legal struggles of these elected officials and listened to many of their constituents who came before them searching for help. I do not remember my opponent, the incumbent of the former District 19, attending any of these meetings. I supposed he obtained his information regarding the needs of the people from other sources.

LaDonna and I tried to attend every community support event conducted within the district. We supported auctions, pancake breakfasts and spaghetti suppers everywhere. The expenditures at these type events are personal expenditures. Most people think campaign funds are being spent, but campaign finance laws prohibit these type expenditures, unless the items purchased are donated back to the organization. We met with and shared our experience and hopes for the future with everyone we met.

I broke down the district by precinct and endeavored to drive to the home of every registered Democratic voter, as indicated by someone who had voted in at least one of the past four elections, every Independent voter, and as many Republican voters as I had personal friendships with. This group of voters covered 75 percent of those casting votes in one of the previous four elections. I spent my weekdays from mid-April through the end of September executing this task. The legal subject of this journal ended my campaign efforts in October 2014. I have no idea how many miles I put on my truck doing this, but I do know this effort allowed me to recognize the needs of the citizens in the district. I gained an appreciation of the impact of the closing of one of the formerly operated ferry sites in Edmonson County. I helped fight the removal of a US Army Corps of Engineers dam on Green River. The removal of this dam would have lowered the water level at the final operating Mammoth Cave

Ferry to a level that might preclude operation of the final ferry on the river operating in the district. Few realized, nor appreciated, the negative impact this would have on the people living in Northeast Edmonson County. Many of the residents of that area felt there were business owners in Brownsville that encouraged the closure of the Mammoth Cave Ferry, in order to force residents to make the trek through Brownsville. While this added forty-five minutes to one hour to their travel time to major medical or hospital care, it might mean some additional money would be spent in Brownsville. I determined an operational ferry or a low-water crossing of some kind must be available at the Mammoth Cave Ferry site. This need remains.

I had the opportunity to meet with residents all over the district and to listen to their needs. I searched for every opportunity for voters to meet me and LaDonna and learn what we had been doing with our lives. I created a web site to share my life's work and my family information. We prepared all the campaign message material except the mass mailing sheets that people normally throw away at the post office. I was advised to take a photo of myself shooting a shotgun, in order to visually announce my support of the Second Amendment. I had served in the military for twenty-eight years, been part of National Guard marksmanship teams winning national pistol and rifle shooting competitions. Why would I need to announce my support of the Second Amendment with a contrived and posed photo?

This brotherhood of candidates, mentioned earlier, became a great source of information on events and community issues. All the Democratic candidates and many of the nonpartisan candidates shared news of coming events with us. We responded in kind where we could. One learns so much more as a candidate than any single individual could ever know. Once people have confidence in your integrity and earnest desire to help their community, they also keep you informed of what is happening in their community.

Governor Beshear, Speaker Stumbo, former Speaker Richards, and many, many of Kentucky's Democratic leaders attended our fundraiser at the home of Roger and Doris Thomas in the late summer of 2014. We had a wonderful final push toward the election in

November. I felt our efforts and our message was receiving much positive consideration throughout the district. Our television and computer advertising was completed and scheduled. We were in the final phase of meeting our election goals. The campaign was completely unaware of the "October Surprise" that was to come! The impact of this surprise will be described in the final chapters. I will only confirm to you now that any "October Surprise," executed in such a way as to cast doubt on any candidate will result in that middle group of undecided voters moving to an opponent. I was unsuccessful in my election effort after October 2014. I did receive almost five thousand votes though, a number that would have won many previous elections in District 19. I attribute this vote count to those citizens and voters who have known me all my life, have served with me in church or in the many civic organizations in the community. These people knew my heart and soul and supported me regardless of what was alleged and reported.

SECTION II

The Indictment, the Trial, and the Outcome

4

AN ATTEMPT TO ASSIST

Like the old soldier of the ballad…an old soldier
who tried to do his duty as God gave him the
light to see that duty.

—General of the Armies
Douglas MacArthur

I began my legislative campaign in full force after the Christmas holidays in 2013. I was in the final week of terminal leave from my job as director. January involved establishing my campaign Web page, opening a campaign account, making initial reports to the Kentucky Registry of Election Finance, and beginning visits and contacts with local and state supporters. The pace was just what I expected, and within a couple of weeks, it just felt like a new job.

I campaigned as a Democrat. My grandfather was a Democrat, my father was a Democrat, and as far as I knew all the members of my fraternal family were Democrats. My mother is a Republican, and her mother's family members (Humphreys) were charter members of the Republican Party from Iowa. I grew up listening to my mother's conservative views and my father's family beliefs that the

Democrat party served the common man. My personal views were hybridized from an early age. When I entered the military and later became an officer, I adopted the view that service members serve the nation and the Constitution, where engaging in campaigns was not only frowned upon; in some cases, it was illegal. During this time, my daughters and my son decided to register as Democrats as well. I have at least one sister and one brother who felt the Democrat party was far too liberal, especially with the spending of taxpayers treasures. My sister changed her party affiliation to our mother's Republican party and a brother initially registered Republican. I only share this to point out that I was an announced Democrat candidate in a year when the Republican Party in Kentucky were eager to claim the leadership of the Kentucky House of Representatives, the last state in the South to retain Democrat leadership. This is not to assert that the United States Department of Justice would target an individual because of their political status, but to highlight the timeliness of the much later indictment and even a trial. In today's world of technology and information sharing, few would accept the idea that something investigated, closed and records maintained and provided to the CID/FBI as a matter of support would be brought to indictment one month prior to an election, from an investigation that had been proceeding for more than a year could be considered pure coincidence.

In late February 2014, I was contacted one morning by FBI Agent Mark Coleman, asking if I would have time to meet with agents and go over some of the Academy operational processes and standard operating procedures related to their investigation of the August 9, 2013 incident. I identified that the new director and staff would have better access to all that information than I would. I would, however, be happy to meet with him at the academy to clear up any issues. Agent Coleman indicated there was no need for me to come to Fort Knox, a 1.5-hour drive, and that we could possibly meet at my home? I indicated that would be fine and asked when he had in mind. The agent asked if "this morning" was okay, and I said sure. I asked when he might arrive, and he indicated in about an hour. As it is about a two-hour drive from Louisville, and a 1.5-

hour drive from Fort Knox, so it now seems he was already on the way when he called. I was in the middle of preparing contact lists for my campaign and felt that I could readily discuss any of the general operations issues from memory.

I welcomed Agent Coleman and another agent into my home, went to my office, and spent about two hours going over the processes and procedures that I and the academy had used during this time. I answered all questions in as clear and direct way as I could because I thought the agents only needed confirming information to make sure they understood the process and how things worked at the academy. I had not referred to my personal e-mail files or logs before they arrived, since I felt I could fill in any gaps they had from memory. My job, as I envisioned it, was to fill in any gaps they were having in the actual material collected from the Academy. It was a very cordial meeting. At no time was I informed that I or any other member of my staff were targets of an investigation into any potential wrongdoing. I felt no reason to suspect that I needed an attorney, though now the timing and location of the visit seems purposely planned to prevent such representation and to supplant any consideration that representation was necessary.

At the end of the meeting, Agent Coleman thanked me for my help and then pulled a subpoena from his coat advising me that I would need to share this same information with the grand jury the following week. I was shocked to receive this subpoena, since I thought the visit was only to fill in their investigative blanks. I was advised that my appearance was just to help the grand jury decide on the outcome of the case. I informed the agent that all I had shared was from memory and that I would refer to my personal records to make sure all comments were completely accurate as I did not want to any possibility that a gap in memory would be construed as misrepresentation.

I went back and reviewed the exact sequence of events leading to my knowledge of the incident, the notification, and my directions to contact the CID. I advised the agent by phone that my review resulted in some minor corrections and that I would bring copies of my e-mails showing the accurate times and processes. I was advised that this was fine.

About a week later and on the day before my appearance date in Louisville, Kentucky experienced a heavy snow and icing situation. I contacted Agent Coleman regarding the appearance time, and he instructed me to contact CPT Milton A. Turner, the Fort Knox special assistant to the United States Attorney and that he might be able to advise me if I could report later than the 10:00 a.m. EST appointment on March 4. I called and CPT Turner advised that if the time indicated was ten o'clock, I should be there at that time. I departed very early and drove on roads that were not completely cleared of ice and snow all the way to Louisville, luckily without incident. I arrived about thirty minutes early, checked in, filed my travel voucher, and was advised to wait in an adjoining conference room until called. I had taken a good book to read, so I began the wait. While I was reading, someone closed the door on the conference room. I later heard the voices of Ms. Kemmye Graves and Ms. Rolanshia Windom outside the conference room. I assumed they were also called to provide testimony. I did not open my door to say hello; I just waited for them to come in and sit down. They never did. At approximately 2:00 p.m., I was notified that I would be next. Captain Turner came in and was very cordial, apologizing for the wait and advising that I should just repeat what I had told the agents.

We entered the grand jury room, and I was seated in a solitary seat against one wall. Captain Turner took a chair at a small table in front of me, with the nineteen jurors on the grand jury being seated behind tables around three walls. At this point, I was sworn into the grand jury and then advised of my rights. Since no one had shared this point, I was taken aback that a witness would be advised of their rights. I assumed that this was to impress upon me the serious nature of the testimony and insure my answers would be the "truth, the whole truth, and nothing but the truth." I still was not informed that I, or anyone other than the primary defendant, was a target of any investigation.

Captain Turner then took on a completely different personality; he was no longer cordial. He seemed agitated and on a mission. I

answered all the questions that were asked as accurately and truth-
fully as I could. While I had expected to answer questions regarding
the allegation of sexual contact against a staff member, the questions
presented were more about my staff, their training, and about processes and procedures for reporting of sexual abuse. I kept indicating
that I had directed the contact of the CID as soon as I was notified.
Captain Turner then gave me documents from incidents of reported
sexual harassment that had been investigated and reported by Ms.
Graves in a previous cycle. I explained what was reported to me and
that I had agreed with her recommendations and resolution of the
matters. Captain Turner then asked why I did not report these sexual abuse incidents. I shared that they were not sexual abuse incidents and had been appropriately investigated. I was then asked if
Ms. Graves was a qualified criminal investigator. I answered, "No,
but she is a state-trained equal employment opportunity counselor
and routinely investigates allegations of sexual harassment." This dialogue of him alleging sexual harassment had occurred and my coun-
tering that it had not continued for some time. He then opened
dialogue regarding whether I had daughters and how would I like
them being involved in an incident like he was alleging. I shared that
such an incident did not happen per the report I received. At some
point, Captain Turner concluded his questions and then asked the
jurors if they had any questions. Several asked questions but seemed
to be upset that we had seemingly not done something they felt we
should have. Two questions even asked if I had done any additional
investigating after the CID was involved. My reply was "No, once we
turn the investigation over to the CID, any involvement by us could
be seen as interfering with the CID investigation". The lady asking
this persisted, and one of the other jurors spoke up to advise her
that the academy could not investigate when the CID was involved.
This stopped this line of questions. At about 4:15 on March 4, all
questions were answered and both I and the grand jury were released.

As I departed Louisville, I felt there was something going on
beside the investigation into the primary allegation of sexual contact. I called my former supervisor in Frankfort, Colonel (Retired)
Michael Jones to advise him of my impressions. I heard later that

he had been subpoenaed to testify as well, and he reported that he was asked similar questions to our processes and procedures. He too felt that the scope of the effort by the district attorney had changed, though in what direction we could not determine.

I remained in contact with other people from the academy and my former supervisor throughout the summer of 2014 to inquire if anything had happened. I continued my efforts to gain election as a state representative, fully expecting that one of my former staff might be indicted at any time. I knew that we had done everything we could and in the exact right sequence, so I was not concerned with any negative impact on me or other staff members.

5

THE CHARGE RELATING TO JANE DOE #1

If you have ten thousand regulations you destroy all respect for the law.

—Winston Churchill

Law applied to its extreme is the greatest injustice.

—Marcus Tillius Cicero

Other than the person alleged to have been involved in the actual accusation of child abuse in our case, six additional people were indicted for "failure to report child abuse" in late September 2014. These include two female cadre. Ms. Rita Carthen and Ms Rolanshia Windom, the assistant female platoon sergeant, Mr. Gabriel Onusko, the commandant, Mr. Leroy Burgess, the Standards and Policy Analyst and Equal Employment Opportunity Commission (EEOC) representative, Ms. Kemmye Graves, and me, John W. Smith, Director, Bluegrass ChalleNGe Academy.

During the first weeks of a Youth ChalleNGe cycle, the young cadets become overwhelmed with the change in expectations regarding their efforts and duties. All ChalleNGe programs around the nation work in a firm and compassionate manner to provide time for assimilation of knowledge and the acclimation to expectations of behavior, leadership and effort. As the program is voluntary, the cadet candidate's assured homesickness results in many pleas to parents to go home. Many who are of legal age (eighteen) actually sign themselves from the program without knowing where they will go after leaving. This well-defined two-week period of general homesickness can continue up to eight weeks after the beginning of the cycle for some applicants.

During the first two weeks of the program at Bluegrass ChalleNGe Academy, staff and cadre demonstrate the behaviors expected by the future cadets in leadership positions. Classes are conducted to explain the concepts of leadership, expectations of the program, educational opportunities are defined, the Test of Adult Basic Education (TABE) is conducted to determine the educational levels of each cadet, physical training begins, instruction on sexual harassment, cadet infractions and punishments, promotions and rewards, etc. are presented. Cadets are monitored and evaluated daily to determine how well they are adapting to the new environment. From these evaluations, the initial cadet leadership is appointed to begin duty in the third week. After this, the leadership changes every two weeks. Jane Doe #1 was a typical cadet in this regard. She was deemed an outstanding leader, and she worked to help other young ladies deal with their homesickness. She was among those chosen for cadet leadership in the first or second iteration of selections. She continued to struggle with her own homesickness issues and wanted to go home several times.

On February 8, 2013, Ms Stewart, the First Platoon Teacher, was approached by a female cadet who stated that several female cadets were discussing filing sexual harassment statements against the platoon supervisor. She expressed that she thought some were claims of inappropriate touching or proximity by the First Platoon supervisor. Ms. Stewart immediately contacted Mr. Gabriel Onusko of the allegations.

Mr. Onusko and Ms. Stewart obtained comments that Ms. Stewart recorded in a Memorandum for Record format, and Mr. Onusko took these statements to 1SG Leroy Burgess. When 1SG Burgess read the comments, they were related as "sexual harassment" allegations; apparently from the earlier briefing that Ms. Graves had provided to all cadets. Ms. Graves had shared with the cadets that they should report anything that made them feel uncomfortable. 1SG Burgess prepared a formal request that Ms. Graves conduct an Equal Employment Opportunity Commission (EEOC) Investigation then tried to contact Ms. Graves by phone to follow up on this request that she conduct a sexual harassment investigation based upon the allegations. Ms. Graves was not in the office on the afternoon of 8 February 2013, but upon receiving word of the allegations; she came into the Academy on Saturday, February 9, 2013, to begin interviews. I was included in the e-mail transmitting the initial request to Ms Graves. I was at home at this time on a regular day off. No action at this point was necessary on my part, as an investigation had been requested by the commandant and it would be performed by the EEOC Representative.

Based upon the transcript of the audio taped interview Ms. Graves conducted with Jane Doe #1, she asked what had happened. After hearing the general description of the incident, Ms Graves went over the three primary questions that would identify potential sexual abuse. During this exchange, Ms. Graves had to define the specifics of each element; since Jane Doe #1 wasn't sure that she understood the meaning of the descriptions. All efforts were made to determine exactly what had happened, relating to the cadets' point of view. Late in the interview, Ms Graves inquired if Jane Doe #1 was homesick and wanted to go home. Jane Doe #1 indicated she was and did want to go home. Ms. Graves tried to tell Jane Doe #1 the advantages of staying and that everyone in the Academy was there to insure her safety. Ms. Graves concluded the interview by asking the cadet to prepare a written statement of her allegation, as none had been prepared to that point. The reporting and investigation process started as a staff initiated response to allegations made during the initial staff interviews. At the end of the EEOC interview, Ms. Graves asked Jane Doe #1 to prepare a statement of the occurrence, as she had not done so yet. The cadet prepared a statement after all the efforts and discussions Ms. Graves had shared to obtain an explanation of the circumstances.

Here is a redacted transcript of that statement:

"Feb. 9, 2013

Incident (Summary) "On Tuesday, I was Sexually Harassed by (REDACTED). He forcefully put my hand on his lower area & it made me feel extremely uncomfortable. It was in the cadre office doorway because he was giveing (sp) me the squad leader arm band thingie. I had my arm extended until he was velcrowing (sp) it together. Then *I moved my right hand to my left shoulder & that's when it happened.* It happened before dinnertime chow." (emphasis added by the author)

When Ms. Graves interviewed others and viewed video surveillance of the floor where this had taken place she determined that the door remained open, that numerous cadets walked by to see what was going on in the room, and that Ms. Rolanshia Windom was leaning on wall opposite the doorway observing the interactions for some time prior to Jane Doe #1 departing the office. Cameras did not have a view within the office. Ms. Graves identified cadets walking by to interview, and especially Ms. Windom as she had directly observed much of the interaction and had witnessed the cadet leaving the office.

From statements, Ms Graves determined that Jane Doe #1 had, on multiple occasions, asked for the squad arm band identification sleeve. The supervisor had not received the new arm bands from the logistics section and when Jane Doe #1 asked again on Tuesday, 5 February 2013, he told her he would look in the office for an old squad leader arm band. She followed him to the room and he had asked Ms. Windom if she had a safety pin (to affix the sleeve to the outside of Jane Doe #1's coat). Ms Windom looked and did not find a safety pin. The supervisor then attempted to tightly affix the shoulder sleeve insignia to Jane Doe #1's arm using the Velcro fastening system. When it was affixed, he asked her to move her hand so he could see if it would stay in place. After she moved her hand, Jane Doe #1 left the office walking by Ms. Windom. There was no sign of distress observed by Ms. Windom or by Ms. Graves upon the video relating to the time of the alleged incident.

This is the view from the hallway in the ladies dormitory where MSG Miller assisted with the request of Cadet Jane Doe #1 for her Squad Leader Arm Band…In her interview with the Academy Equal Employment Opportunity Commission representative she indicated she was standing "by the door" while he complied with her request…This is the view that PSG Windom also had before MSG Miller completed the task and when Cadet Jane Doe #1 exited the room after MSG Miller attempted to place the defective arm band on Cadet Jane Doe #1's right upper arm…In her statement to the EEOC representative, PSG Windom stated, "On Feb 5 I was in the hallway of the Cadre office and SGT Miller and (Jane Doe #1) were inside and I did not see anything out of order…SGT Miller came out and ask me for a pin…(Jane Doe #1) did not seem to be upset."

This is the view of the portion of the dormitory floor where platoon discussions took place and where the platoon gathered prior to going outside in inclement weather...The alleged incident occurred on Tuesday, February 5, 2013, at approximately 1800 (6:00 pm. EST)...The door to the right center of the illustration is the door represented in illustration 1...The leftmost door is the entrance to the stairway from the third floor...Cadets were gathering for the evening meal when Cadet Jane Doe #1 asked for an arm band and assistance from MSG Miller...PSG Windom was also on the floor and assisted MSG Miller at one point by trying to locate a safety pin at the small desk at the left edge of the illustration...During the very short time she was at this desk, there were female cadets passing by the open door in illustration 1 going to and from the female latrine which is the first door down the hallway on the right (not visible in the illustration)...It is not clear whether the center door in this illustration was open or not...The area behind the viewer and over your left shoulder is the open bay sleeping area containing double bunks for approximately thirty cadets.

This is a view of one of the two security cameras located just above the cadre door in question...One of the two cameras is visible in illustration 2, just above the door...These two cameras were approximately eighteen inches apart and faced in opposite directions to cover all the space below them...One faced the cadre desk and the open bay barracks and the other faced the hallway...This security system provided a thirty-one-day digital record of everything occurring within the camera view...There was no camera inside the cadre office, nor facing inside the office...This system is what the EEOC representative reviewed to ascertain as much as she could regarding the statements of MSG Miller, PSG Windom and Cadet Jane Doe #1...Her impressions, based on experience, the statements and the expressions she witnessed on the video led to her conclusion and verbal report that "contact, if contact occurred, was accidental."... Based on this conclusion, and the formal agreement of all parties in the outcomes recommended, the EEOC representative felt no need to prepare a copy of the viewed video to attach to the record report.

Title IX, that federal program that is widely known regarding the requirement for female sports in schools, applies to all National Guard Youth ChalleNGe programs as well. Title IX also requires certain steps to be conducted in all school sexual harassment investigations. In many Kentucky schools and universities, the Equal Employment Opportunity Commission Representative conducts these Title IX sexual harassment investigations. In the Title IX required mediation session relating to this incident, and after the completion of the investigation, Ms Graves explained the incident, the location, the situation, the dress of both parties, the openness to both casual observance and actual adult witness involvement. Ms Graves advised all present that she found no evidence to validate the allegation. Ms. Graves shared with Jane Doe #1 that she was not saying that her account of the incident was not true; rather, she had found no evidence to indicate anything other than accidental contact had occurred. From this session Ms. Graves developed a recommendation agreeable to both parties and that both parties signed. This document would afterward be shared with the director for approval. Jane Doe #1 indicated this outcome was fully acceptable, both initially and during the later meeting with the director.

Ms. Graves did the same with a second cadet who had alleged that unwanted contact by the supervisor had occurred as he was pointing to her computer screen while standing behind her. She alleged that he had "rubbed himself on her shoulder" as he accomplished this maneuver. Ms. Graves interviewed this cadet twice. The first interview involved the cadet's explanation of what was alleged to have happened in the classroom. At this time, the teacher and all the female cadets were present and working in the classroom. Ms. Graves conducted a second interview after reviewing videos of multiple days' activities in the classroom. She was confronted with the video evidence that the supervisor was never behind her in the classroom and that the only potential opportunity for him to have touched her in any way was when he had sat beside her, leaning over to take a photo of the computer screen with his cell phone. While they could not see any contact, it was concluded that his knee might have touched her knee, but they could not see it. During the interview with the supervisor, he produced the computer screen image on his cell phone. It was a math problem that he had sent to his son in college for help. He showed his son's reply, which he had shared with the cadet. The cadet then indicated that the supervisor just seemed to violate her "space."

I was at a national inspection of the Appalachian ChalleNGe Academy in Harlan County, Kentucky, at the time of Ms. Stewart's hearing of the incident. Staff and cadre followed academy and state policy in conducting an initial inquiry, obtaining and conducting an investigation into alleged sexual harassment. Commonwealth of Kentucky and Department of Military Affairs procedures exceeded the requirements set by Title IX in these investigations. I returned to work on Monday, February 11, 2013, and was provided a verbal explanation of the allegations while Ms. Graves concluded the investigation. On February 13, 2013, Ms. Graves provided a final report of incidents she had investigated. Her report indicated no substantiation of either alleged event, but she recommended some conditions the supervisor should follow in the future to lessen the likelihood that any other allegations could be brought to bear. Both cadets agreed to the conditions and the supervisor, while indicating he had done nothing inappropriate but would sign the document if that is what was required to end the situation. All parties in the investigations were brought to my office after signing the findings and recommendations of the EEOC representative. I asked all of them if the investigation and outcomes were satisfactory. Their signatures indicated a willing concurrence of this, so I asked if each were aware of their rights to appeal the results of this investigation to the Department of Military Affairs. No one indicated any negative response. I asked Ms. Graves if all the recommendations were completed. She indicated her recommendation for a local letter of reprimand had not been completed. I directed that it be completed that day and that she notify me when it was finished. She did so.

Within one week of the alleged incident, Jane Doe #1 became eighteen years of age. At this point, she could self-terminate from the program at any time. Her family came to the Academy that weekend for a "birthday party" for her. She continued and graduated approximately seventeen weeks later. During the cycle, the First Platoon supervisor was also our softball coach. Jane Doe #1 was our star softball player. Under the leadership of the supervisor, Mr. Onusko and the female cadre at the time, this group of young ladies became the first platoon in the history of Bluegrass ChalleNGe Academy to graduate with every cadet achieving either level III rank or honor platoon member status. At the end of the cycle, I always asked the graduates to share their impressions of the program and to make recommendations about how I can improve the program. I do not require the cadets to sign their responses, though many did so. One of the questions asks the cadet, "9. Which Cadre or Staff member from the entire program (AMP, Cadre, Platoon Sergeant, Medical, Teacher or other) would you like to recognize for their positive influence in your life (only one please)? "Jane Doe #1 listed" (REDACTED)" (the Platoon Supervisor). The next question stated, "What made them better?" Jane Doe #1's response was; "He wouldn't let me just quit the program even though I could have left anytime I wanted."

Every person in this chain of events did exactly what they were trained to do. Ms. Stewart was told by a cadet that other cadets were discussing filing sexual harassment charges against the supervisor. She responded immediately to something that caused her concern. She contacted Mr. Onusko to help interview and record comments, as the supervisor was the subject of the allegations. They both took these allegations to 1SG Burgess, who reviewed and asked Ms. Graves to investigate and directed that the supervisor not approach the platoon until the investigation was completed. Ms. Graves came in on a Saturday and began the investigation, talking to cadre and cadets and reviewing the recorded video. She finished her investigation by talking to the supervisor on his first regular day back at work. He worked with the male platoons until after the final mediation session, the confirmation session in my office, and the completion of all recommended outcomes. Ms Graves formalized the report and obtained agreement in the outcome from all parties, presenting the final report to me on Wednesday.

This entire academy effort, from start to finish, is exactly what Title IX expects to happen. Both claimants continued and graduated the program, both at the highest rank. No other sexual harassment or retaliation allegations occurred. During 2015, I requested the Department of Education, Office of Civil Rights (DOE, OCR) conduct a compliance review of this investigation, as they have overall responsibility for Title IX sexual harassment investigations. After receiving no response from DOE, OCR I sent a second request, this time including Congressman Brett Guthrie as a recipient. I then requested to visit the congressman to explain the issue. This meeting, with staff, resulted in the congressman's indication that he could not become involved in the criminal case, but he could inquire why DOE, OCR had not responded to a request by a constituent. Several days later, I received a call from DOE, OCR regarding my inquiry. The representative stated that DOE, OCR only conducted compliance reviews of DOE schools and that Youth ChalleNGe was not a DOE school. I acknowledged that I understood that the executive agency listed in the law that was directly responsible for Youth ChalleNGe was the Department of Defense (and National Guard Bureau as a sub element), but that Title IX indicated DOE, OCR had the ultimate responsibility for compliance. He indicated that DOD would have to conduct any compliance review performed. He then asked if this had answered my questions. I indicated I understood what he had indicated. He asked if I had any other questions, and I responded by asking if he could respond formally to my letter. He seemed perplexed but indicated that he would. I have never received that formal response.

In the incident relating to Jane Doe #1, it is noteworthy that Ms. Stewart was the first person to become aware of the allegation and was the witness when Mr. Onusko took the statements, yet she was not charged in the indictment. Title IX grants immunity to that person making the initial report. This seems to indicate the prosecution was aware of Title IX requirements, as 42 USC § 13031 makes no such provision. Additionally, I do not think Ms. Carthen was ever mentioned in the discussion of the Jane Doe #1 investigation, and I am unsure that she was even on shift during this time, yet she was indicted by the prosecutor and grand jury regarding the failure to report child abuse in the Jane Doe #1 incident. There was an allegation made during the investigation that Ms. Carthen and Ms. Windom had asked the cadet not to talk about the investigation. I do not think this happened as implied, but regardless, this was not a "failure to report" issue. During Ms. Graves's interviews relating to all investigations of any kind, witnesses are admonished to not discuss with their fellow cadets or staff anything that is asked or answered during interviews. This precludes potential other witnesses from comparing statements and precludes ill feelings between cadets on the floor regarding conflicting points of view during investigations. If Ms. Carthen and Ms. Windom expressed any admonition regarding discussing the investigation, I am confident it was along this line. While the prosecutor implied that this was to keep the cadet from talking to her parents, the tape recorded transcript of the interview proves Ms. Graves encouraged Jane Doe #1 to advise her parents of the incident.

It is my belief that the prosecutor desperately sought any potential evidence that the supervisor had been involved in previous instances of behavior that would point to a pattern of criminal behavior. After being advised by Ms Graves that she had conducted an investigation of alleged sexual harassment during a previous cycle (class), the FBI then requested all the investigation files Ms Graves had conducted, and they settled on this one to tie to the subsequent charge. There is no evidence the FBI or the prosecutor ever interviewed Jane Doe #1 prior to December 2013 and only used the comment "forcefully put my hand on his lower area" from Jane Doe #1's statement as the basis for pursuing the charge and indictments. From this one expression on a statement, completed after Ms. Graves investigation was completed, came charges that have put a stain on the records of six faithful and caring employees of Bluegrass ChalleNGe Academy, and resulting in the final three employees still at the academy being terminated based solely on the completion of the prosecution's "investigation." I suspect each of the six have spent an average of $10,000 or more in legal fees to clear their names.

This charge of "failure to report child abuse," Section 18 United States Code § 2258 is a federal class B misdemeanor. Three employees of the Department of Military Affairs were terminated based upon the conclusion of the "Investigation." How many other employees of the Commonwealth of Kentucky are at risk, if the only thing required to be terminated is the completed investigation into the charge of a misdemeanor? The potential punishment for this federal class B misdemeanor was increased by legislation to "$100,000 in fines, one year in prison or both." I hope you realize the trepidation of employees who felt they were doing exactly what was expected, were then charged 18 months after the incident, and were abandoned by their employer without even an internal review into the allegations.

In early June 2015, the assistant district attorney for the Western District of Kentucky offered a pretrial diversion to any persons charged in a misdemeanor in the case. The offered diversion included "fifty hours of community service," paying "$100" restitution by each to Jane Doe #1 for alleged counselor expenses relating to the incident, not committing any additional crimes for one year and reporting to the United States probation officer during the period. (This was later changed to calling the assistant district attorney [Ms. Gregory] four times during the year.) At the end of the diversion period, the charge would be "dismissed, with prejudice," meaning it could never be brought up again. There is an expectation that the charge will also be expunged from the person's legal history at that time. The agreement further required each charged person to sign a document, and in my case, the document stated, "It appearing that you have committed an offense against the United States, in that on or about February (either 8th or 12th), 2013, you failed to report to social services or law enforcement facts that gave you reason to suspect a child had suffered an incident of child abuse."…Had I been in the possession of any information that caused me to even suspect an incident of child abuse had occurred, I would have contacted the CID immediately, just as I had in every previous occurrence and in the occurrence that led to the backward review.

Five of the six codefendants in the misdemeanor case accepted the pretrial diversion. I moved forward to prove my innocence and to insure all this information is included in the trial record of February 2016, three years after the alleged event. The results of that trial will be shared later in this journal.

I urge you to research and read academic papers written to share the current injustice connected with our grand jury system. The federal grand jury process requires radical change. Some states have changed their grand jury process to come in line with all the various recommendations. I will be working to encourage Kentucky to become one of the leaders in this effort.

6

PREPARATION FOR TRIAL

Preparation is the be-all of good trial work.
Everything else-felicity of expression, improvi-
sational brilliance-is a satellite around the sun.
Thorough preparation is that sun.

—Louis Nizer

The preparation for trial consumed most of my time from the end
of the campaign in November 2014. As a retiree, I could have just
cocooned myself with my computer and worried regarding the
expected trial. If a person is involved in their community, this cannot
happen. After the election, I continued duties at Oakland Baptist
Church as a Sunday school teacher for the Adult II Class and helped
with our annual Widow and Widower Christmas Banquet. I continued service as a member of our trustee committee and performed
duties as our church moderator during monthly business meetings.
In May 2015, our church body selected me to serve as an active deacon within the fellowship. In late 2015, I was selected as a part of,
and then to chair, our church Pastor Search Committee.

My other community activities did not slow down either. I remained an active member in the Smiths Grove Lions Club and in July 2015 became the treasurer for the club. I continued my service with the Warren County Cattleman's Association but declined a request to join the board in early 2015. I continued as the commander of the Fort Campbell Chapter of the Military Order of the World Wars but will end that term of service in 2016. I joined the Bowling Green Chapter of the Military Officers Association of America in 2015 and was asked to serve as a committee of one regarding nominations for officer positions. I continue as a life member of the Veterans of Foreign Wars and a member of the Bowling Green America Legion Post. Each of these organizations is focused on the helping of others within our communities. I am proud of my membership in each.

As I indicated earlier, Ms. Graves, Ms. Windom, and Mr. Burgess were notified of their separation from the Department of Military Affairs in March or April 2015, with their termination citing the "completion of a United States District Attorney investigation." I am happy Ms. Graves chose to execute her prerogative to appeal the separation, though the outcome was unsuccessful. The entire Youth ChalleNGe staffing effort in Kentucky is fully or partially funded through federal/state cooperative agreement as non-merit positions (classified as Non P-1). These positions are fully vested state positions, with salaries commensurate with their job classifications, receiving medical benefits, workman's compensation, retirement, etc. The only difference in a Non-P1 and a P-1 (Merit position) is that the Non-P1 position is an "at will" position. Non-P1 employees have no recourse if they receive a "services no longer needed" letter. The only time an appeal is allowed is when the release is for cause. Since the Department of Military Affairs chose to include the reason for the dismissal on the letter, the three terminated employees had the ability to appeal.

Our trial date was originally set for December 2014, at our initial arraignment in October. My attorney, Mr. Darren Wolff, shared with me during our appearance at the bar to plead "not guilty" and that this was just to set a date and that a December trial would not provide Mr. Miller's defense time to prepare. Mr. Wolff predicted a March 2015 date as a reasonable date to consider. The actual date became June 22, 2015, instead of the initial December, 2014 or the expected March 2015 date. Mr. Wolff and I had three or four meetings in his office between October 2014 and May, 2015 to discuss the case and the potential outcomes. I shared that I would accept a complete dismissal of charges but preferred a trial and a "not guilty" verdict. Without a trial, none of the situational evidence regarding the academy efforts with Jane Doe #1 would ever be included in the public record. Unfortunately, none of this situational evidence would ever be presented.

In May 2015, the prosecution "superseded" the charges against Mr. Miller. Two charges were dropped completely. The charge relating to the forcible sexual relations with Jane Doe #3 was dropped, along with another charge relating to her. The new charge seemed to indicate Mr. Miller has encouraged the victim to engage in some sort of sexual performance as a commercial enterprise. The mandatory minimum incarceration moved from two years to twenty years. What seemed odd regarding this change was the implied agreement of the prosecution that any sexual act that was alleged was moved from forcible to consensual. While there were no charges against any other academy staff in this case, we all had to return to the federal courthouse to enter our plea of "not guilty" in the case of Jane Doe #1 again.

At the time the charges changed against Mr. Miller, the defense needed an extension to prepare for this change in charges. I had encouraged my attorney to stand firm on the June date, since we all wanted the charges related to Jane Doe #1 separated from the Jane Doe #3 case. It seemed all the other attorneys for the other misdemeanor defendants wanted to delay their trial. Mr. Wolff indicated that it is second nature for a defense attorney to accept a delay in trial as it usually benefits the defendant. I was disappointed when we were the only holdout in accepting the delay and finally consented, only because no one else wanted to continue to trial apart from the other allegations. What made this exercise so strange was that some of the other attorneys had filed a motion early in the process to separate the misdemeanor from the felony charges. These motions were denied by the court. At a juncture in the process when Mr. Miller's charges in Jane Doe #3 were changed and there was an unmistakable opportunity to separate the different allegations, as was earlier desired, everyone caved in to request the extension.

In June 2015, Ms. Gregory, the assistant United States attorney, distributed an opportunity for a pretrial diversion to all the misdemeanor defendants. As the process continued through June, some of the conditions changed. The conditions requiring reporting to and following directions of the United States probation officer changed to only calling Ms. Gregory quarterly.

Three of the defendants chose to accept the pre-trial diversion when it was initially offered; Ms. Graves, Ms. Carthen, and Mr. Burgess. I assume each were tired of the process, tired of the continued turmoil in their lives, tired of the continued payments to their attorneys, and enticed to agree to a process that would end the ordeal within one year. This would result in the charges of "failure to report child abuse" being "dismissed, with prejudice," meaning the charge would be dismissed and could never be brought up again. Each were told that at the end of a year the dismissal would mean they could honestly answer that they had neither been convicted nor charged in the case.

Mr. Onusko's opportunity to meet with his attorney regarding the diversion was delayed a couple of weeks. Once he was aware of the details of the diversion, though he fully maintained his innocence, he also agreed to the process. He wanted to get the ordeal behind him and move on with his life. Mr. Onusko had served his nation with distinction and had retired from the United States Army. He shared with me that he had never even received a traffic ticket before this allegation. Each time our misdemeanor group diminished, my opportunity for a successful outcome also diminished. I cannot fault any of my codefendants for their personal actions in the case.

After a couple of messages with Mr. Wolff; I commented that I would accept no pretrial diversion that required me to sign a document stating, "You failed to report to social services or law enforcement facts that gave you reason to suspect a child had suffered an incident of child abuse." Neither I nor any of my staff in the case regarding Jane Doe #1 had done anything of the sort. I had no facts that gave me reason to suspect that anything inappropriate had happened. Each member of the staff involved had acted in good faith to report the verbal allegations of sexual harassment of female cadets up the chain. Mr. Burgess had immediately requested that an investigation into the allegations be conducted. Ms. Graves had come in on her day off to begin the requested investigation. She finished the investigation two days later and made her official report and recommendation to me the next day. I considered her report and asked both parties if they were happy with the investigation and the outcomes recommended. After hearing their affirmative responses, I verbally approved the report and the recommendations and insured that the recommendations were carried out. Ms. Graves filed the report, and the class continued. My record, like that of Mr. Onusko (with the exception of my one speeding ticket), was unblemished. I never had reason to suspect a child had suffered an incident of child abuse regarding Jane Doe #1; and in both previous and subsequent instances when I thought the allegations indicated such, we immediately contacted the Fort Knox CID. Why would I sign a diversion document that was a lie? I assume lying to a federal judge or assistant district attorney is a felony??

At this juncture, Mr. Miller continued with his felony charges, and only Ms. Windom and I were proceeding to trial to prove our innocence.

On July 21, 2015, I visited Mr. Darren Wolff to discuss our preparations for trial. We spent the afternoon going over discovery and having discussions of policy and jurisdiction and peripheral issues. Mr. Wolff gave me a copy of a new superseding information, another change to the charges on the indictment. A superseding information is different from a superseding indictment because no grand jury action was required. As indicated earlier, this agreement was between the prosecution and defense attorneys in the case. It required no consultation with any grand jury and was the final action against Miller.

As I reviewed the new document, I realized that there were four counts listed, all against Mr. Miller, and they all were listed under the same primary indictment number as before. My first question when Mr. Wolff indicated there was a new supersession was "When do we have to appear before the federal magistrate again to plead 'not guilty'?" Mr. Wolff indicated we wouldn't have to appear this time since we weren't named in the newest supersession. I then asked, "Why did we have to appear before, since none of our charges changed?" I then asked, "Since I was charged in the previous indictment (same case #) in Count 2, and now Mr. Miller is charged in Count 2, how would the jury distinguish between defendants for consideration of Count 2?" At this point, we both became aware that the indictment only having one defendant listed could mean there would be no case against us in court—if no other supersession occurred. It seemed a cruel means of indicating that a decision had been made to dismiss charges against Ms. Windom and me. Mr. Wolff began looking into this prospect quietly. He found that I remained charged under the superseding indictment and not the superseding information; therefore, this was also much contemplation for nothing.

Mr. Wolff also indicated the new supersession may be to adjust the charges against Mr. Miller in line with a potential plea agreement that he, the public defender, and the ADA had negotiated. This new supersession added a fourth Jane Doe to the list. As I considered the charge relating to Jane Doe #4, I realized this new count related to an investigated case of reported sexual harassment that had occurred and had been investigated at the same time as Jane Doe #1. While completing the fact finding in the Jane Doe #4 allegation of contact while Mr. Miller leaned over Jane Doe #4 in the classroom from behind Jane Doe #4; Ms Graves and Mr. Onusko reviewed video recordings of the day Jane Doe #4 indicated the alleged incident occurred. It was very fortunate that one of the classroom cameras had Jane Doe #4's computer and seat center screen. Viewing the entire day, Mr. Miller was never behind Jane Doe #4. The entire previous day was viewed, and Mr. Miller was again never behind Jane Doe #4. The next preceding day was viewed, and Mr. Miller was never behind Jane Doe #4. At this juncture, they shared their findings with Jane Doe #4. Mr.

Miller was seen to be in the classroom helping cadets. He was seen helping Jane Doe #4. The only time Ms. Graves indicated there may have been contact was an instance when Mr. Miller pulled up a chair to sit beside Jane Doe #4 and point at her computer screen. *If* contact occurred, it could only have been his knee touching her knee. Ms. Graves's report on the alleged incident did not find any indication that any contact had occurred, but she did indicate that Mr. Miller should maintain the three-foot rule distance from female cadets.

I found it interesting that any consideration of Jane Doe #4 had been omitted from the original indictment and the initial supersession. No indictment was forthcoming from either grand jury action. It seemed that only after there was a potential plea agreement in play, that this count against Mr. Miller was added to the indictment. I go back to my earlier explanation of the power of the prosecutor. This new charge was simply added by the prosecution at the point a plea agreement was expected.

I told Mr. Wolff on July 22 that I felt the charges against Ms. Windom and I would absolutely be dismissed. I remain confident in the investigation Ms. Graves conducted and knew there was no indication of anything inappropriate occurring between Mr. Miller and Jane Doe #1 or #4. If Mr. Miller agrees to a plea agreement, like the other 89.55 percent of people charged in federal courts, the ADA probably does not want any information added to the record that would indicate his innocence. This is a sad commentary on our system of justice. It was also an overly confident expression on my part.

Ms. Windom finally agreed to the pretrial diversion after getting some of the wording changed. She asked that language be included to indicate that this agreement in no way precluded her from being rehired at Bluegrass ChalleNGe Academy. The prosecutors agreed and added the language. Neither they nor her attorney shared with Ms. Windom at the time that the federal government could not dictate to the Commonwealth of Kentucky their personnel hiring practices. What Ms. Windom intended for good turned out to be just so many words on a document. She deserves to have her job back at Bluegrass ChalleNGe Academy if she wants to work there now; but the language on her agreement meant nothing toward that end.

7

THEN THERE WAS ONE

Those who stand for nothing will fall for
everything.

—Alexander Hamilton

On August 28, 2015, the United States Attorney's Office for the
Western District of Kentucky distributed their final pretrial news
release regarding my case. The release was primarily to announce the
plea agreement between the government and the attorneys of the primary defendant. One readily sees the apparent secondary reason for
the release in the inflammatory expression in the inclusion of my case

Close examination of this release reveals its misleading purpose;
it is a carefully worded instrument to cast continuing doubt on the
innocence of any person involved in this case. At the time this was
released, only one defendant in any of the allegations combined in
this indictment continued to fight these allegations. I am happy that
my attorney and I came to an agreement that we would fight this to
the end. Mr. Wolff's former military background gave him special
insight into what was being alleged. The press release is indeed fac-

tual, but with facts that lead the casual readers down a completely different path.

The platoon supervisor was a former police officer. His job title at Bluegrass ChalleNGe Academy did not classify him as an administrator. He was a cadre supervisor, in charge of the cadre who worked for him within his element of the program and responsible for the female platoon. He did plead guilty in a plea agreement worked out by his attorney and the assistant district attorney. The fact that this is a superseding information indicates this. You see, he was initially charged in an indictment (handed down by grand jury action), and his charges were changed the first time by a superseding indictment (another grand jury action). The final change, the superseding information is an action that did not go before the grand jury; rather it was an agreement worked out among the attorneys involved.

The primary charge against him was lowered to a Commonwealth of Kentucky Revised Statutes charge of sodomy in the third degree. This final charge surely was the result of a plea bargain deal between his legal representative and the office of the US Attorney. Why was a Kentucky Revised Statutes charge used instead of a federal statute, since the entire process had been handled under the provisions of a special maritime district or military installation statutes of the federal government until this time? The Supreme Court ruled in *Lawrence v. Texas* in 2003 that it is unconstitutional to bar consensual sex between adults, calling it a violation of the 14th Amendment. There are apparently no sodomy charges currently in the federal statutes, or if there are the provisions of age of consent or special circumstances are not listed. It seems that Kentucky law addresses the age of consent in sodomy as under the age of eighteen; further defining roles where one party is above the age of twenty-one and in a position of authority.

As far as the other three incidents are concerned, counts one and four resulted from allegations made by female cadets six months earlier in the staff directed sexual harassment investigation. The supervisor being charged in relation to Jane Doe #1 during the initial indictment and the superseding indictment (grand jury actions) based on a single allegation also resulted in six other staff members of Bluegrass ChalleNGe Academy being charged with the failure to report child abuse misdemeanor. The count relating to Jane Doe #4 was added during the final superseding information. Jane Doe #4 was never included in any indictment as a result of grand jury action. Both these incidents were investigated at the time by a dedicated and competent Commonwealth of Kentucky Equal Employment Opportunity Commission representative. The report of this investigator indicated, in both instances, that any alleged contact, if it occurred at all, was inadvertent and accidental, occurring during the conduct of normal and routine activity.

The event under one allegation (Jane Doe #1) occurred in a staff office, with open doors and in view of other cadets and staff. It occurred as the platoon supervisor, at the request of the cadet, was looking for an insignia of rank worn on the outer garment. When he found the insignia, he attempted to help affix it to the young lady's upper right arm. The second allegation (Jane Doe #4) occurred in the female classroom, with his being called by Jane Doe #4 to assist with a problem on her computer. In this case, he apparently sat beside the cadet to look at the computer screen. This occurred while class was in session, with all cadets and the female instructor present. When the incident was investigated, the review of the classroom cameras clearly indicated the cadet's study station. The camera clearly showed the supervisor being called to assist the cadet. It showed him pulling an empty chair and sitting just to the cadet's right at her work station. It showed him lean across the desk with his cell phone and take a photo of her computer screen. The investigator reported that if there was contact, the only contact could have been his knee touching the cadet's knee or leg. Again, this was ruled as inadvertent or accidental contact associated with the conduct of normal activities.

The investigator did require the supervisor to apologize to both young ladies for what they thought happened and required him to receive a letter of reprimand. These actions were not meant to be punitive in nature; rather the expression of seriousness of interactions between a male supervisor and a female cadet, especially when a female instructor and a female cadre were present to assist. At the time of these two allegations, they were the first instances I am aware of that the platoon supervisor was involved in any negative allegations or any kind of investigation.

The release goes on to point out that he worked for the Leitchfield Police Department and "resigned the position following complaints of inappropriate conduct toward two women." After we requested the CID investigation in August 2013 into the allegation of sexual contact against the supervisor, information gathered by the FBI was shared with us. This information indicated there were two allegations of inappropriate behavior against him. During a police department investigation into one of these matters, Mr. Miller was apparently suspended for two weeks. He apparently chose to appeal this decision with the chief of police, and the suspension was changed to one week. There is a second appeal indicated, with no outcome listed. Approximately one year later, there is an indication of an EPO against him by his wife during a time of separation or divorce proceedings. There is an indication by a state review panel that all the allegations against him were without merit and that he should be returned to full-time status. At some later time, during a discussion regarding shift assignment, he requested a third shift assignment (so he could participate in his children's sports activities) but was given a second shift assignment (a shift that precluded any involvement with his children). Based on this shift assignment, he chose to resign from his position with the police department. Mr. Miller did resign, and this was following (by one year) the allegations made against him.

The Office of the United States Attorney indicated the maximum potential penalty of the law in his case. In this same characterization, they chose to include me, as the final misdemeanor defendant seeking to prove his innocence, by including me in the press release and announcing the maximum potential penalty that could be imposed.

Finally, in a complete demonstration of the seriousness of this case, it is shared that the United States Attorney has assigned two assistant district attorneys, involved the weight of the Federal Bureau of Investigation, and the investigative resources of the United States Army Criminal Investigation Detachment toward bringing this final misdemeanor allegation to justice.

After this release, only one media outlet in Kentucky picked up the information of the release in its entirety. *The Daily News* in Bowling Green ran the story, adding to the information that John Smith was a candidate against Michael Meredith in the last election, ignoring his party's request to step down from the race due to the allegation and declaring his innocence. WBKO, the local television outlet, did not run the story and only shared the Miller plea on their web report. The local Public Television Media outlet ran a condensed version of the release and did add John Smith in a one-line comment.

Many interesting things resulted from the concept and organization of the trial proceedings. During the initial efforts to gain an indictment through testimony before the grand jury, Captain Turner asked over and over if Ms. Graves was qualified to conduct a criminal investigation. I affirmed that to my knowledge she was not, nor would I ask her to conduct a criminal investigation. He completely discounted her role as an Equal Employment Opportunity Commission representative and her ten-plus years of experience conducting investigations. He completely discounted her personal role as a foster parent and her training and work with the Kentucky Department of Community Based Services in that role.

As the trial progressed, the assistant district attorneys seemed intent to show that at least one of the requirements of the government under 42 USC § 13031 (a 'designated agency') had been met. They introduced a Memorandum of Agreement between Fort Knox and the Kentucky Department of Community Based Services in Elizabethtown, Kentucky. This document included signatures of the Fort Knox Garrison Commander, the Ireland Army Community Hospital Commander, a representative of the Kentucky Cabinet for Health and Family Services, and a local representative of the Kentucky Department of Community Based Services. There was no signature from a Bluegrass ChalleNGe Academy (BCA) or Kentucky Department of Military Affairs representative. BCA was not mentioned anywhere in the document. The federal statute, 42 USC § 13031, was not mentioned anywhere in the document. The local Kentucky Department of Community Based Services is the same organization Ms. Graves worked with as a foster parent and many times inquired to regarding her EEOC investigations. It seems so incredible now that that same agency later identified as the "designated agency" is also a state agency without criminal investigative authority. This same "designated agency" under the stipulations of the law (42 USC § 13031) is that agency where "known or suspected child abuse" is reported. An employee for DCBS evaluates the investigation, determines its validity, and *then* notifies criminal authorities *if* the reported child abuse is validated. What was different regarding the investigation of DCBS (another state agency with no criminal authority) and the Title IX authority vested within Kentucky Youth ChalleNGe?

I remained in the fight in order to show these logical discrepancies for what they are. I could have taken the minimal pretrial diversion and paid the one hundred dollars, showed that I had completed fifty hours of community service (I regularly perform 150 hours or more each year for community, church, and service organizations), and had all charges dismissed, never to be brought up again. That our legal system provides such a miniscule penalty as an incentive (one I probably should have accepted) relating to a charge so widely stressed in the media seems absolutely perverse on its face. Once this perverse incentive is declined, then the entire legal system seems to work to insure a conviction in the case, lest any future defendant be so bold as to challenge the system.

These two particular instances are widely held as two of the primary changes that must be made to the processes of grand jury deliberations. Many other recommendations for change are being proposed by legal scholars throughout our nation.

8

THE TRIAL

The greatest dangers to liberty lurk in insidious
encroachment by men of zeal, well-meaning but
without understanding.

—US Supreme Court
Justice Louis D. Brandeis

Final preparations for the upcoming trial included meetings with my
attorney, payment for an investigator to meet with a former cadet
who, in a statement during our initial 2013 sexual harassment investigation, said that the cadets making the complaints had lied regarding their statements. My attorney advised that it was unwise for me
to talk to this former cadet in any manner and that my wife should
not correspond with her either. Mr. Wolff recommended I pay a private investigator to conduct interviews and arrange for the former
cadet to testify. This young lady confirmed her statements and told
us she was willing to testify to that in court. A subpoena was issued,
and she reported to court, only to be excused that day by my attorney
without testifying. (It made me wonder why I spent the investigator
funds in order to line her up.)

As we prepared for the trial, the district attorney moved up the dismissal of all the other codefendants, who took the offered pretrial diversion, to the week prior to trial. At this point, I advised my attorney to inquire if the pretrial diversion offer was still in place. I fought in this case for two primary reasons. I have never knowingly done anything wrong, and I remain convinced that the former BCA staff indicted with me did nothing wrong in this case either. I wanted to continue the fight to prove this position for each of us. Once the probation was concluded and the charges dismissed on all these former defendants, I felt they were now able to share that their charges were dismissed without trial. This is absolutely a true statement. My attorney was told no, regarding the pretrial diversion though maybe in more graphic and colorful language.

LaDonna and I reported to Louisville on Monday at 9:30 a.m., February 15, 2016, for the final pretrial conference. Magistrate Judge Lindsay covered all the "logistics" of the trial and went over his rulings of all the motions before the court. Most of the meeting went as we expected. Judge Lindsay stated that he felt the trial should take no more than three days to empanel a jury, present the prosecution, and then present the defense. He asked the prosecution if they felt they could meet this burden. They indicated they felt their prosecution would be finished NLT noon on Thursday. We departed Louisville with an expectation that all would go in an orderly fashion.

Wednesday morning, February 17, had been set for counsel to meet with Judge Lindsay at eight thirty in the court library to discuss final issues. The prosecution wanted to introduce a photo of the respondent in the primary case (from his driver's license), but Judge Lindsay denied this request, stating it looked too much like a mug shot. At this time, the fact that this defendant had agreed to a plea agreement in all alleged incidents was not to be mentioned in my case. It had no bearing on the case. These final discussions lasted past ten o'clock so we entered the courtroom behind schedule.

Judge Lindsay conducted the voir dire from the bench with counsel for the state and my attorney listening to every reason any particular juror expressed in answer to his questions. This process went on and on before the Judge empanelled twelve jurors and the required alternates. This was more than the usual six jurors empanelled in a federal misdemeanor case, but I was told this was too our favor as only one person had to remain steadfast to a not guilty opinion to result in a hung jury, and a hung jury in a misdemeanor case was as good as a not guilty verdict. I felt good about having the additional six jurors. This too turned out to be a false sense of hope.

The trial began with both the prosecution and defense giving their opening arguments to the jury. The prosecution used the statement indicating Jane Doe #1 was "forced to touch the respondent's penis" over and over during the opening. From their comments, one would have thought this supervisor had taken the cadet into a room, had exposed himself, and forced her to fondle his exposed genitalia. The jury at this point had no indication that the young lady had asked for the supervisor's assistance in putting a uniform accessory on over her winter coat just before departing to go outside for the evening meal at the dining facility in another building. There was no indication that the supervisor also had on his uniform and winter coat. The jury was not informed that all the other young ladies were standing in the third floor assembly area watching and waiting. There was no reference that the door to the cadre office remained open. No one pointed out that a female cadre was posted in the hallway, just outside the doorway and witnessed the final few minutes of the assistance effort, stating in a later witness statement that she saw nothing inappropriate happen nor did she notice any unusual expression on the face of the cadet when she departed the room. The jury was only forced to hear "forced to touch his penis" repetitively.

During my attorney's opening, he went over all the things regarding the alleged incident that the prosecution had left out. He covered my spotless military record and described my community involvement. As he considered how to end his opening he stated that "during this trial we will show you that absolutely nothing criminal occurred" during that incident in February 2013. This was a big mistake, and one my attorney had gone over with me many times. We had no need to prove that nothing happened—we only needed to prove that I had no knowledge of anything happening or no reason to suspect that anything happened. There is a very subtle difference in these two views. At the point my attorney made his statement, the prosecution immediately objected, and the group approached the judge. His ruling on this point put my attorney on his heels and probably made our case much more difficult to secure a not guilty verdict. During the pretrial conference, the judge had not allowed the prosecution to bring the respondent's plea agreement into the current trial. What the primary defendant admitted to in a plea agreement situation had no bearing on my case. When my attorney indicated "we will prove that nothing happened," he opened the door for the prosecution to get the agreement (or at least that part relating to Jane Doe #1) admitted into evidence as a "fact" that something had indeed happened—and he pled guilty to it. Judge Lindsay agreed with them, and not only was the jury informed that someone had pled guilty to "forcing Jane Doe #1" to touch their clothed penis; this same statement was also placed in the jury instructions. From the voir dire process, I do not know if any of the members of the jury had ever served on a jury before or not. I am confident that they did not realize the full implications that the respondent pled guilty to the "touching" of Jane Doe #1 in order to obtain a far reduced charge in a later incident relating to Jane Doe #3 (the incident that occurred approximately six months later, and one where I directed that CID be involved immediately upon hearing of the allegation).

We ended the first day after this, with Judge Lindsay excusing the jury after the federal court house was closed. Everyone had to exit the building through a side door.

We began day 2, after the judge ruled on the motion from the day before. We started late on day 2 as well. The prosecution called Jane Doe #1 to the stand to provide an account of what had happened in February 2013. She reported to the stand in a slow, deliberate, and downtrodden state, dressed in black and not making eye contact with anyone. She began by answering the prosecution questions in a quavering voice and after three or four questions sank into the obligatory cry. Once the court had taken a few moments for her to recover and provided a tissue, this damp overture was concluded and was never repeated. At the urging of the prosecutor, she described what she alleged happened in February 2013. The prosecutor at one point asked the witness when she told her parents about the incident. She started to reply, "It was just after I received the le——" when she was abruptly interrupted by the prosecutor. A restated question from the prosecutor was "I guess I meant, Did you tell your parents after you graduated from BCA?" She then replied, "Yes". I suspect that the uninterrupted answer would have been "It was just after I received the letter from the FBI regarding the investigation." At the time, I did not know why the prosecutor did not want this to be before the jury.

My attorney then had a chance to conduct a follow-up—though it was after 4:00 p.m. by this time. He went through several questions regarding the academy, her involvement there, her achieved rank, and her graduation. On multiple occasions, the witness asked my attorney if he could repeat his question. On multiple occasions, she asked that he repeat questions up to four times. He went over the process where the incident was reported by the teacher and Mr. Onusko after another cadet had alerted them and they had interviewed her. He went over the actual timing of the investigation and that the report was concluded the following Wednesday, only four working days after the initial reporting. He went over that she had been briefed on the outcome of the report, the recommendations the respondent would have to follow, and that she agreed to these recommendations in writing. She then was asked, "After you had signed the report, were you taken to Colonel Smith's office for him to go over the recommendations?" She indicated "Yes". "Did Colonel Smith read over the recommendations in front of everyone?" "Yes." "Did Colonel Smith ask everyone if they signed the report and that their signature indicated they agreed with the report?" "Yes," "Did Colonel Smith inform you that you had the opportunity to appeal the report at any time and provide the contact information to you?" "Yes."

The prosecution later came back and asked the witness why she agreed to the report in Colonel Smith's office? She indicated at that time that "I just wanted the whole thing to be over." She was asked if she ever described what she had alleged to have happened to Colonel Smith at any time. She indicated "No".

My attorney then returned and gained concurrence of the fact that the witness graduated the program. He gained concurrence of the fact that the witness played softball for the academy and that the respondent in the sexual harassment investigation was the coach of the team. The witness was then asked to review and identify a personal end of course evaluation she prepared for Colonel Smith in the last week of the program. She stated it was her evaluation (though grudgingly—as it was not signed). On this evaluation, the witness had completed approximately three pages of questions. On question 9, she was asked to identify that single staff or cadre who was the most positive influence in her life while at the academy. She had named the respondent in the sexual harassment investigation as that person. Question 10 asked why. She stated on the form that "Because he knew that I could go home at any time and would not let me quit."

I had conducted these evaluations with every class since my second class at the academy. I used the answers to get an impression of what cadet graduates felt about all areas of the program, what they felt about the losses we experienced during their cycle, and how I could reduce overall losses. I asked how each cadet graduate felt about how BCA could reach more at-risk youth. I asked for them to name both the "most positive" and the "most negative" staff or cadre with reasons for each candidate. I explained if there is no one that comes to mind just write, "NONE." I used these nominations to publically recognize all those persons receiving positive votes during graduation. The top individual received a plaque for himself or herself, and we posted a duplicate award on the wall in their platoon area. I only allowed cadets in the room with me when we completed these forms. I did not want any staff or cadre walking around looking at what cadets wrote or trying to influence their nominations. I did not share these evaluations with anyone after the graduations either, only the compiled results. Jane Doe #1 had indicated during the questioning that she was "told by a cadre what to write on the form." This was impossible, since there was no cadre in the room and the form must be completed in some manner before the cadets left the room. Logically, since the cadre knew that every cadet's positive nomination would result in those names being shared during the graduation ceremony, why would any staff or cadre want a cadet to write someone else's name? The jury, at this point, looked like they had completely seen through the earlier defeated display by the witness and understood that she was less clever with her answers and urgings to repeat questions than she intended.

My attorney then asked if the witness had become eighteen years of age on the Saturday following the completion of the investigation. She indicated yes. Did you know that you could self-terminate (sign yourself from the program) at that time? She answered, "Yes, but he wouldn't let me go home." My attorney asked, "Who wouldn't let you go home"? She answered with the name of the respondent in the sexual harassment investigation. My attorney followed with "What do you mean, he wouldn't let you go home?" She responded, "He just wouldn't let me go!" At this point the jurors were shaking their heads.

The prosecution covered a couple of points in redirect, and I thought I had made clear to my attorney that the witness went home on three separate times after the investigation was completed. BCA always had an Easter pass and a Mother's Day pass in the early cycle, and the third pass was either at week 7 or Memorial Day, depending on where Easter fell in that year. Jane Doe #1 spent a total of seven plus days at home after the investigation was completed. She could have remained at home and never returned if she wanted. She always returned. My attorney did not choose to address this when he went back following the prosecution redirect. I have no idea why he felt this unimportant. To me, it would have made the witness's statements regarding "He would not let me go home" absolutely ridiculous.

The prosecution called the father of the witness. He was asked by the prosecution to describe why his daughter had come to the academy. He responded that it was probably his and her mother's fault, because they had always given in to whatever she wanted. He stated his daughter was a senior in high school but would lack two credits graduating at the end of her senior year. This situation would cause her to graduate a year later with her little sister, and she did not want to do that. Jane Doe #1 had found out about Bluegrass ChalleNGe Academy through her school counselor, and together, they felt she could attend and complete her hours through our credit recovery program and graduate with her peers. He indicated she had been a star softball player throughout her school career, but an injury had meant she would be unable to play her senior year. My later understanding was that she had broken an ankle, and it was pinned together. This was not shared with us until after our entrance physical was completed, when she asked for an ankle brace on the second or third day. She told the nurse that she had one at home and her dad would bring it in. Later in the cycle, she was completely cleared for physical training and even started on our academy softball team.

Several things were strange regarding his testimony of her status. He indicated she would require only two credits at the conclusion of the senior year, yet after trying the credit recovery program for a short time, she asked to change her educational component to the GED track. As she was eighteen by that time, she could make her own decisions regarding the educational component. She completed the program but did not successfully complete the Official Practice Test (OPT) in order to attempt the GED while at the program. Another complication occurs with the father's testimony, though it was not identified until after the trial. Jane Doe #1 had been asked about her softball prowess. She stated under oath that she "came from the womb with a bat and glove.". BCA had been told of this exceptional ability and that she was being scouted by university coaches. This was also testified to by her father. After the trial, an Internet search was made of the North Bullitt High School website. On that site, all the softball players are listed for each year. Jane Doe #1's name is nowhere on the roster. Her little sister's name appears, but not hers. Maybe the university coaches were observing her during to her summer travelling team efforts? Maybe they were unconcerned that she had a pin in her ankle? I will leave it to each of you to consider these questions, just as I have.

The prosecutor then asked if the director had ever called to advise the parents of the incident where she had been "forced to touch the respondent's penis." He indicated no one had ever called him or the mother. Of course, what was left out at this point was that an investigation had been completed that indicated that "contact, if contact occurred, was accidental." There is no need to call parents every time accidental contact occurs. The prosecutor did not ask the parent when the cadet told them about the incident.

My attorney followed up with the father on a couple of general issues and then asked if he had ever talked to Colonel Smith. He indicated that he had. My attorney asked, "How many times?" He indicated, "At least once." My attorney asked if this one time was during the class intake briefing where the director addresses all the parents. He indicated yes. My attorney then ended his cross-examination of this witness, as there was nothing else to be gained from him.

The next witness was Special Agent (SA) Mark Coleman, Federal Bureau of Investigation, stationed at Fort Knox. SA Coleman had multiple purposes for the prosecution. He testified about his interview that he conducted at my home in February 2014—one year after the sexual harassment investigation, two months after I had retired, and at the beginning of my campaign for state representative. SA Coleman also read excerpts from my grand jury testimony, approved by Judge Lindsay, to the jury. SA Coleman then filled in any blanks regarding the complete investigation and all the things the FBI had uncovered during the investigation. SA Coleman was very exact in stating that we had conducted a sexual harassment investigation and that our investigator was not qualified to conduct a criminal investigation. Both truthful, and both unrelated to each other. He read into evidence the appropriate statutes from 18 USC § 2258, which was the basis for the misdemeanor charge. He indicated that this charge came from law and from 42 USC § 13031. And he finally indicated that 28 CFR 81.2 also provided clarification to the statutes. He defined the extensive evidence that the FBI had collected in the case and the extensive interviews that were conducted. He defined the grand jury process and read the portions of my grand jury testimony allowed by Judge Lindsay. SA Coleman was a very creditable witness whose demeanor was exactly what one would think an FBI special agent should portray. His prosecution testimony had lasted from approximately 2:00 p.m. till 4:00 p.m.

that day. Remember that the prosecution had indicated they felt they would be completed NLT noon on Day Two.

My attorney then took over the cross-examination of SA Coleman. He asked when the FBI became involved in the case. SA Coleman indicated he thought they were involved on the second day of the investigation, as I had directed the CID be called. My attorney asked when they took over the case, and SA Coleman did not know the exact date. I had dealt with CID SA Kyle Buckout from August 2013 on the later allegation and continued to deal with him until November 2013 when he advised me the CID had gone as far as possible with the case and that I would be dealing with SA Coleman, of the FBI from this point on. My only interaction with SA Coleman, after being notified by CID SA Buckout reported the change in status, was to provide copies of five or six individual cadet records requested by SA Coleman. I had them copied and scanned and sent them to him on the same day he requested them. I retired at the end of December 2013 and advised SA Coleman that he would be dealing with my successor after that. My attorney questioned whether SA Coleman had testified that the FBI "discovered" the record of the previous sexual harassment investigations relating to the respondent. My attorney then asked SA Coleman if the possibility of previous sexual harassment investigations was made known when Ms. Graves had volunteered that information to the CID during their initial interview with her. SA Coleman responded that she did volunteer the information. My attorney then asked that the discovery of the document was from the voluntary suggestion of the academy investigator. Agent Coleman responded that it was, but that it may have resulted from the CID questioning. My attorney went on to ask just how extensive was the material the FBI had collected in the case. SA Coleman responded that there were about fifteen boxes of material. My attorney asked how much of those fifteen boxes had been copied and provided by BCA staff at the request of the FBI. SA Coleman responded, "Most of it."

As Mr. Wolff was running out of factual direction with SA Coleman, my attorney asked if "Colonel Smith had invited the FBI into his home upon being asked and answered all their questions at that time. Agent Coleman responded yes. My attorney asked if SA Coleman had always found Colonel Smith to be cooperative and truthful. SA Coleman responded yes. Mr. Wolff then asked, "Did you ever have any indication that Colonel Smith or anyone else was involved in a conspiracy to cover things up in this case?" SA Coleman responded, "There was one indication of this." I sat straight up in my chair, and my attorney asked, "Who gave you this indication?" SA Coleman then responded that there was one instance when he was involved in a telephonic communication with Frankfort where a conspiracy seemed to be alleged. My attorney persisted, "Who were you talking to?" SA Coleman responded that he was not sure, but remembered that this person had shared that another person had told him of a conversation where another person reported they heard a state employee declare that the defendant would have "top cover." Mr. Wolff persisted toward obtaining a name, and SA Coleman stated he thought the caller's name was Sikes or Seitz. I immediately recognized this person as a National Guard JAG officer serving the adjutant general. I had no idea why he would be involved in this case because the legal representative of the program was the attorney representing the Department of Military Affairs and not the National Guard. Mr. Wolff asked if this conversation was recorded. SA Coleman responded, "No." SA Coleman had already responded that special agents were prohibited from audio or video taping interviews without the expressed approval of the Special Agent in Charge (SAC) in Louisville. There were no recordings of any of the interviews conducted by the FBI in the case. Mr. Wolff then persisted, "When did you go to Frankfort to interview Mr. Seitz?" SA Coleman responded he did not go to Frankfort to interview Mr. Seitz. Mr. Wolff then asked, "So you did not obtain the names of the persons who overheard the comments alleging someone else had indicated Colonel Smith would have 'top cover'?" SA Coleman responded he did not. My attorney then persisted, indicating, "So with all the 'extensive investigations' the FBI had already conducted in this case, you did not feel it warranted travelling to Frankfort to follow up on this conspiracy or cover up as you said?" SA Coleman responded, "No" My attorney also followed up with asking, "You did not even feel it important to contact the SAC to get approval to check out a tape recorder to take with you to Frankfort?". SA Coleman again responded, "No."

Again, at this time the entire jury seemed to be shaking their heads at this testimony. It was again late in the day when the judge excused the jury. Day 2 was over, and the prosecution had not rested yet. We had one more day of scheduled trial time. Judge Lindsay asked the prosecution how much longer they would require. They indicated they felt their final witnesses would not take long to conclude.

The final scheduled day of trial opened with the prosecution asking Judge Lindsay to allow them to recall SA Coleman to the stand to "correct the record" on his testimony. Judge Lindsay allowed this non-standard request after gaining the approval of my attorney. The prosecution asked SA Coleman if he had reviewed his notes regarding the call referred to on Thursday. Mr. Wolff had asked SA Coleman on Thursday if he had his notes with him, and he responded that he did not. That they were apparently on a flash drive and not with the prosecution team seemed incredulous at the time. Only the people in the courtroom realize why I say this. The prosecution team carried six to ten large boxes to the courtroom each day. They came into the room with rolling brief cases. Of the four prosecution team members present, there may have been three laptop computers present. With all this supposed "evidence" against me at their table, the only thing missing was the thumb drive SA Coleman had his investigative notes on? SA Coleman responded that he had reviewed the notes. When asked what he had learned from the notes, SA Coleman responded to the effect that the call from Seitz had occurred discussing many issues ongoing between the FBI and the Kentucky National Guard. At one point in the discussion, Mr. Seitz had indicated he was present when the direct supervisor of the Kentucky Youth ChalleNGe effort had taken a call from one of the directors regarding the request from the FBI to produce copies of all student and staff records at the academy (the fifteen boxes previously mentioned). SA Coleman indicated that Seitz shared that the supervisor had a cavalier attitude about the request and had said that the programs would have "top cover" relating to the request. SA Coleman then indicated that this conversation regarded a situation that had occurred after Colonel Smith had retired and involved his successor. It is important to note that the witnessed conversation did not involve the circumstances related to the incident; it involved the requirement to copy and provide all student and staff records available.

My attorney on his cross-examination then asked SA Coleman to restate his responses to all the questions relating to the willingness of Colonel Smith to invite two special agents into his home, answer all their questions honestly and without any reservation, and that *now* SA Coleman had no reason to suspect that anyone had ever engaged in any effort to hide or cover up anything related to these investigations. SA Coleman responded to the effect of "That is correct." I admired SA Coleman for digging through his notes and coming to the stand to "correct the record" regarding the earlier statements. I do not think the prosecution found this in any way supportive of their case. I often wonder if the average citizen would have the opportunity to correct the record, or if they would be charged with perjury.

The prosecution then brought forward four witnesses whose sole purpose was to testify that there was no record that BCA had contacted their organization in February 2013 regarding the sexual harassment incident. A representative of the Fort Knox CID was called to testify. A representative of the Fort Knox Military Police Station was called to testify. A dispatcher from the Elizabethtown post of the Kentucky State Police was called to testify. And finally, a representative of the Kentucky Department of Community Based Services (DCBS) was called to testify. My attorney had no questions for any of these witnesses. Since this was approaching midmorning of the final day, my attorney probably should have risen at the beginning and openly stipulated that we agreed that no reports of any child abuse had occurred, as the sexual harassment investigation conducted by a Commonwealth of Kentucky Equal Employment Opportunity Commission representative had concluded and reported that any contact, if contact occurred, was accidental. Accidental contact requires no reporting to outside agencies. Looking back, Mr. Wolff could have conceded that no calls were made to anyone, since based on the report of accidental or inadvertent contact, if contact occurred at all, there was never a need to contact anyone. We could have ended the prosecution's waste of our valuable time.

The prosecution also introduced a Memorandum of Agreement between Fort Knox and the Elizabethtown Department of Child Based Services (DCBS). They portrayed the document as that document required by 42 USC § 13031 to identify the designated agency for Fort Knox. That this document did not even mention 42 USC § 13031, nor did it mention BCA, and that it was signed by the Fort Knox Garrison Commander and Ireland Army Community Hospital and two state representatives made no difference to the court in their accepting the document for that purpose. The law requires the attorney general or her representative to identify the designated agency for the particular federal land. The attorney general has a representative on all military installations to handle legal matters there. A JAG officer is sworn in by the attorney general as a deputy assistant United States attorney for Fort Knox. It would seem that this individual, or a previous individual holding this position, would be the appropriate representative of the attorney general to enter into an agreement with DCBS regarding designated agency responsibility.

The prosecution finally rested at approximately 10:00 a.m. on day 3 of the three-day trial. We had seven character witnesses ready to testify on my behalf at the courthouse and scheduled to arrive by eleven. I had two other witnesses present, but my attorney did not want to call them at that time. Ms Graves was there to testify to her investigation and what she reported to me. Mr. Onusko was there to testify to his part in the process from start to finish and to corroborate witnessing Jane Doe #1 ask the platoon sergeant to help her with her squad leader arm band again, immediately after leaving my office after the final question and answer session I conducted.

We began with our character witnesses. Those testifying on my behalf included:

Dr. Mary Benson, my dentist, fellow church member, and employer of my wife for twenty-eight years, testified to her knowledge of my work within the military, the community, and the church as well as who I am as a father and as a husband. During my many assignments within the Kentucky National Guard, I had chosen the difficult option of becoming a geographic bachelor when I worked away from home. During one of these assignments with the 138th Field Artillery Brigade in Lexington, Kentucky I had the very distinct pleasure to board with Dr. Benson's mother. Each day, after work, I came home to a home-cooked meal and some very pleasant conversation of family, Lexington and Cynthiana, Kentucky where Ms. Henson was born. Dr. Benson's family grew up with our family, and she knows my non-military traits as well as my mother.

Major General Michael W. Davidson, a Louisville attorney and the adjutant general of Kentucky at the time I deployed with my battalion to Operation Desert Storm, spoke on my behalf. General Davidson gave some powerful and moving testimony, though testimony of this sort is very limited in its scope. As an attorney, General Davidson knew exactly what he could say and how he could maximize the impact of what he said. General Davidson was much more than the adjutant general during his time in Frankfort. He asserted his will on our state National Guard force at a time when we had no real estimate of the threat Iraq would become. He challenged leaders at all levels to push to model the very best qualities of leadership. He required his full-time battalion and brigade leaders to attempt and hopefully complete the US Army air assault course. I completed the course with a distinguished group of cohorts. We had one brigadier general in our class, multiple colonels, and an active duty senior army advisor. Major General Davidson prepared Kentucky National Guard battalions and brigades for war. I was both honored and privileged to command the only Kentucky National Guard Combat Arms Battalion mobilized and deployed to the war in Iraq. We were one of only four National Guard combat arms battalions mobilized and deployed from our nation.

Major General Donald (Donnie) Storm testified next. General Storm and I had been battalion operations officers at the same time. He served in Kentucky's infantry battalion, and I served in one of our field artillery battalions. I followed Lieutenant Colonel Storm as the operations officer of the Kentucky Military Academy when I returned from Desert Storm. Colonel Storm had been my personnel officer when I was the chief of staff of the Kentucky National Guard, and I had been his Youth ChalleNGe Director while Major General Storm was adjutant general. Our friendship and close working relationships have covered a lifetime of service and support.

Brigadier General (Chaplain) Patrick Dolan testified on my behalf. He had known me since my battalion days when he answered a smaller call to serve soldiers in the Kentucky National Guard and within the 1st Battalion, 623rd Field Artillery. Chaplain Dolan had become the Kentucky state chaplain when I first became the Youth ChalleNGe director. Before I retired from Youth ChalleNGe, Chaplain Dolan became the National Guard Chief of Chaplains. He holds multiple doctorates and remains a humble servant of our Lord. When I named my son John Patrick, Chaplain Dolan took great pride in his name, indicating I must have named Patrick in his honor! I pray that Patrick continues to be a man after Chaplain Dolan's heart!

Colonel Joe Warren testified next. Joe is a Vietnam veteran, and was my first battery commander when I was commissioned a lieutenant. Joe is the gentleman I replaced in the full-time operations office when I became a full-time soldier in 1980. He was a constant advisor and mentor in the field artillery. Joe commanded Kentucky's 2-138th Field Artillery when my battalion was sent to Desert Storm and was the state recruiting and retention manager when I became chief of staff. Joe's son came through Officer Candidate School while I was at Kentucky Military Academy. Joe and I served as the first placement coordinators for Kentucky Youth ChalleNGe. Joe grew up on a farm in Taylor County, Kentucky, and we shared our lessons learned from our farm years on many occasions. Joe and Judy Warren are dedicated Christian leaders and of the finest moral fabric Kentucky has to offer.

Lieutenant Colonel Jim Cook testified next. Jim is another Vietnam veteran and someone I knew throughout my service in the field artillery. Jim was a recruiter for me when I became director of Bluegrass ChalleNGe Academy, later becoming the program's admissions, mentoring, and placement manager before he retired. During his time of service, Kentucky Youth ChalleNGe transitioned to a program that consistently met or exceeded our admissions and graduate goals. Jim and his team were responsible for my success at Bluegrass ChalleNGe Academy. Jim is also another farm product from Northern Kentucky. We shared the trials and joys of caring for family. Jim and I both lost parents near the same time.

My final character witness was Command Sergeant Major Eddie Satchwell. CSM Satchwell and I worked together at the 138th Field Artillery Brigade. He was one of the most dependable NCOs I have ever known, and our close work in Lexington only paved the way for future team roles. When my battalion was mobilized for Operation Desert Storm, we deployed with the 196th Field Artillery Brigade from Tennessee. CSM Satchwell volunteered to deploy with that unit so he could help support our Kentucky battalion. He was not the only person to do this! During my time as the operations officer and commandant of the Kentucky Military Academy, CSM Satchwell was the state school's manager. The Total Army School System was adopted by the Army, and CSM Satchwell and I worked on National Guard groups to implement the program nationwide. We continued our side by side association when I was the chief of staff, and he became the Kentucky State Command Sergeant Major. CSM Satchwell worked for several years as one of our Youth ChalleNGe admissions, mentoring, and placement coordinators and also put his computer skills to good use helping organize and train mentors on the nationwide reporting system.

Command Sergeant Thomas (Tommy) Pendleton was the final character witness scheduled to speak on my behalf. On the morning of this phase, Tommy was stricken with a stomach virus and could not travel. I came to know SSG Pendleton at my first officer posting. He was an M-110 howitzer section chief when I reported as a brand new second lieutenant. SSG Pendleton was also the Kentucky state trooper in the area, when he wasn't performing National Guard duties. He, his wife, Connie, and his two daughters became dear friends over the years. 1SG Pendleton was my first sergeant when I became battery commander of our firing battery. I had hoped 1SG Pendleton would follow me when I went to battalion headquarters, but others had different plans for him. He became the field artillery brigade command sergeant major ahead of his peers and shortly thereafter became the Kentucky state command sergeant major. He welcomed me to my duties as chief of staff, and we shared many difficult situations. Major General Russ Groves, CSM Pendleton, and I were attending a TRADOC event at Fort Leavenworth, Kansas, in the summer of 1996. Major General Groves was looking for a new chief of staff, and I had heard that my name was mentioned. I prepared a letter telling Major General Groves that I was content to remain the commandant of Kentucky Military Academy as I felt there were several more qualified officers within the Kentucky National Guard than me. CSM Pendleton saw me give Major General Groves the letter at breakfast and asked what I had done. I explained my letter. CSM Pendleton laughed and told me that I had just insured that I would be Kentucky's next chief of staff, as that was exactly the kind of person Major General Groves wanted for his Chief. CSM Pendleton joined Kentucky Youth ChalleNGe as a recruiter. He was there to welcome me to that organization as well, and he remains active as an admission, mentoring, and placement coordinator. Tommy Pendleton, like many of those speaking on my behalf, is not only a military leader and a community leader; he is also a worker and leader for Christ in his church and through mission efforts throughout the country. I have had the opportunity to share many discussions about faith and service with him over the years.

The comments of these exceptional citizens, friends, soldiers, and leaders were both heartwarming and embarrassing. One hopes his fellow man has good things to say about him. We all say we would rather hear these things while we are living, but I will tell you I cried while listening to these dear friends share their comments, even as limited as the court allowed their comments to be.

After my character witnesses concluded, Judge Lindsay took a more appropriate lunch break for the jury. My attorney indicated at that moment that he was ready to go directly into closing after the court reconvened. Everything the prosecution had presented had been countered effectively, the jury seemed to be with us at this point, and anything I may have offered might only confuse the jury regarding the matter at hand. I agreed with his point of view and consented to this course of action.

Judge Lindsay had two open motions to consider, and he apparently decided to do this during the lunch break on day 3. The problem was that his consideration of these motions lasted until about 3:00 p.m. He ruled against us on one of them and did not rule on the final motion. All the time he was ruling, the jury had to wait in another room. This had happened many times during the trial, but mostly because of prosecution motions. When the jury and the judge came back into the room, we moved forward with the closings. The prosecution went first, my attorney second, and the judge allowed the prosecution to go last, as a very short rebuttal to the defense closing.

During the closings, the prosecution returned to their use of the language (modified slightly) by making mention to the "forcing of the cadet to touch the clothed penis." They were allowed to mention that the respondent in that investigation had admitted guilt. They constantly pointed to me and indicated "the defendant ordered the investigation," indicating I knew what was alleged. This was in fact false—as the investigation report, available to the jury, had the written request by the commandant to the EEOC Representative to conduct an investigation. How the prosecutors were able to point over and over to indicate "he ordered the investigation" was disconcerting. I had the feeling that they seemed to be painting me as Colonel Jessup in *A Few Good Men*, as the person who "ordered the Code Red."

My attorney got up and made a valiant effort to highlight that the prosecution had only proven that I was aware of a sexual harassment investigation after it was completed, that all parties had agreed to the recommendations of that report, that I had asked them to verify their concurrence, advised them of their appeal rights, and had monitored the outcomes of the post investigation impacts. He reminded them that everyone who had appeared as character witnesses and even the FBI had commented regarding my truthfulness and leadership. When he closed, I felt as though the jury understood everything.

The prosecution came back with the same though slightly modified "was forced to touch his clothed penis" over and over. They postured that the jury had heard about my truthfulness, stating that since I ordered the investigation, I must have known about the allegations. They went over and over this again and far exceeded the time I thought Judge Lindsay had allowed for that final closing. I was still happy with the trial at this point.

Then the jury instructions were read. This was one point that Judge Lindsay had been considering before the closing. He ruled that a statement of the respondent pleading guilty to the charge relating to Jane Doe #1 would be included in the jury instructions. He then began the reading of the jury instructions to the jury. Near the end of the jury instructions, he told the jury that to find me guilty of this misdemeanor, they must find unanimously. This was what I understood, and I relished that there were twelve jurors in this misdemeanor trial. He then added that to find me not guilty, the verdict must also be unanimous. This comment was not expected. He admonished the jury that the verdict must be unanimous regardless of what their verdict was—that they were to find me guilty or not guilty of failure to report. Four agencies had testified that there was no report, and someone had pled guilty to child abuse. This must have put the jury in a very tight box. This is the problem with strict liability crimes in our state and nation. I still felt that one or more of the jurors understood that they had the power to hold to a conviction of not guilty and that the case does not have to be either/or—that there is a middle ground where one or more feel strongly regarding the case. After considering the case for two hours, the jury came back with a unanimous guilty verdict.

Looking back, should I have testified in my own behalf? Yes, is the answer now. Should I have brought Ms. Kemmye Graves to the stand to testify to her report to me, where she reported that she felt the incident was accidental and incidental contact? Should I have asked Ms. Graves if she told me that any "contact, if contact occurred, was accidental?" Yes, is the answer now. Should I have put Mr. Gabriel Onusko on the stand to testify that he witnessed Jane Doe #1 ask the respondent to adjust the armband on her sleeve immediately after she left my office after the final discussion; that he advised Ms. Graves of this immediately; that Ms. Graves had indicated that only confirmed her initial assessment? Yes, is the answer now. At that time, I had no doubt that the jury, or at least two or three jurors had seen through all the testimony. It was not to be.

Throughout all this effort, I had tried to prove my innocence. I knew, and know still, that I always did what I felt to be right, with the best outcomes for cadets and staff considered. I had dismissed staff before and after this incident who did not measure up to the high standards we demanded. I had terminated cadets for infractions that were clearly beyond any expectation of leniency. I had given cadets second and third chances when I felt termination was not a potential outcome they had considered at the time of their actions.

I remain convinced that no person should be charged or convicted when action was taken by experienced people in an incident and when said investigation produces a reasonable and acceptable outcome. Just because someone else can allege a different outcome expectation based on a law that was not known by those conducting the investigation is no reason to proceed with prosecution. The representative of the attorney general on Fort Knox also had the requirement to identify the designated agency to all covered professionals, to provide a reporting format, and to provide periodic training. Each of these elements should have been considered before bringing charges. The US district attorney hid these requirements from the jury, protested their being considered as elements of a potential crime, and to my knowledge has still not corrected the failure to meet this statutory burden on Fort Knox. This inaction only indicates that they are apparently happy to criminalize a broad range of apparently innocent behavior. If a criminal investigator became aware that an allegation was made and no action was taken, then there may be grounds for charges. That an organization responded immediately, taking the action it knew to take and then the leadership of that organization accepted the recommendation of a veteran investigator, should never result in criminal charges.

9

THE SENTENCING PROCESS

Right, as the world goes, is only in question between equals in power, while the strong do what they can, and the weak suffer what they must.

—Thucydides

This is a court of law, young man, not a court of justice.

—Oliver Wendell Holmes, Jr.

After the court verdict in February, we returned home to await sentencing and to consider what to do regarding the trial. LaDonna and I were so disappointed in the outcome; especially after I had relinquished my right to testify. The sentencing was set for Thursday, May 19 at 9:30 a.m. in Louisville. We continued our community, church, and family work.

Many of our friends and former coworkers, our church members, and soldiers attended the trial over the three days. Mr. Wolff felt confident, as always, because this was just a misdemeanor. I had never been involved in a negative incident in my life, and my life's work seemed a body of work worth considering. Mr. Wolff felt I might pay a fine and be sentenced to probation. As April concluded and the Presentence Report (PSR) was received from the probation officials, I became more optimistic in Mr. Wolff's assessment. The initial PSR score for me was 6, and this is the very lowest score possible in the federal presentence process. From the reading of the report probation could be considered from 0–6 months, and a fine from $500–$5000. No discussion of restitution had occurred and was not included in this report.

In order to insure Judge Lindsay had good reason to consider the minimum sentence or fine recommended, I asked friends and relatives to write letters to him urging the same. I asked that these letters be mailed to my attorney, Darren Wolff, so he could consolidate them into a packet for presentation to the court. Ninety people, from Oregon to Virginia, wrote letters on my behalf regarding my character, my work ethic, my Christian witness, and my family and community involvement.

Within a week of the release of the PSR from the probation office, the United States attorney wrote a presentencing memorandum relating the same story they had used before. They included one argument relating to the score. They indicated that I "should have known" Jane Doe #1 was a vulnerable victim. This one addition to the PSR raised the sentencing guidelines 2 levels. What do two levels mean in this case? It increased the probation period from six months to one year and doubled the potential maximum fine to from $5,000 to $10,000. They also asked that I be held jointly and severely liable for restitution in regards to counseling incurred by Jane Doe #1, and paid by her family, after she graduated.

I prepared a defendant's motion and submitted to Mr. Wolff after receiving this document. Mr. Wolff improved my document and submitted it to Judge Lindsay on the Monday, along with eighty-seven of the letters, prior to the sentencing hearing (I have included a copy in the bibliography). We had received an updated PSR from the probation office the week before developing our response to the prosecution document. The updated PSR had already incorporated the prosecution's recommended two-level increase. Please keep this in mind for later.

On Thursday, we arrived at the federal courthouse about forty-five minutes prior to the sentencing. Approximately twenty-five to thirty friends travelled from southern Kentucky to be there for my support. I had always tried to be cordial and friendly with the staff at the courthouse and was pleasantly surprised to be greeted at the second floor security station with a very friendly "Good morning, Mr. Smith.". I had not been in the courthouse for three months, yet this gentleman remembered me and spoke kindly to me. I very much appreciated and thanked him for that gesture.

After comments by both parties and an opening by Judge Lindsay, Mr. Wolff jumped right into the restitution issue. He restated the concerns stated in our defendant's PSR memorandum and also shared that I should not be punished beyond my fellow misdemeanor codefendants just because I had chosen to avail myself of my constitutional right to a jury trial. Ms. Gregory responded that I had been offered the same pretrial diversion that my codefendants had agreed to, and going to trial was my choice. Mr. Wolff responded that Ms. Gregory knew very well that I had offered to accept the pretrial diversion before the beginning of the trial (after all my former staff had their charges dismissed), and that offer had been rejected.

At this point, pro and con arguments of the two-level increase were discussed. Judge Lindsay indicated he had reviewed both arguments, presented by memorandum, before agreeing that the increase was justified. At the time, before a sentence was handed down, no further arguments could be presented to the judge. What created much consternation and disbelief is the fact that the probation office had changed their PSR recommendations, incorporating the two-level increase, before we ever submitted our memorandum. How, or more aptly asked, why would the probation office or the judge make a change based on the presented argument of the prosecution alone? Was it preordained that our argument had no possible merit?

After all discussions were presented, Judge Lindsay adjourned the court to retire to chambers to consider the sentence. At approximately 10:45, he returned to the courtroom to share his decision.

As a way of prefacing his final sentence; I want to share what the prosecution asked for in the case:

- Thirty days of home detention
- $10,000 fine
- Joint and severe liability for restitution identified

Mr. Wolff had asked for the following:

- Probation, if the court felt probation was necessary
- No fine
- Restitution in the amount of $100, to match that of my co-misdemeanor defendants
- Community service as defined by Judge Lindsay

Judge Lindsay's announced sentence included:

- One year of probation
- Ninety days of home incarceration, and that he would favorably consider waiving the remaining probation after the completion of the home incarceration
- $10,000 fine
- Joint and severe liability for restitution identified
- That I would be able to continue to travel to care for my mother during the periods from 6:00–9:00 a.m. each morning, except Sunday.
- When asked about my ability to attend church, to perform my moderator duties, or my deacon duties; Judge Lindsay replied, "Absolutely not." I think there was a collective gasp from everyone in the courtroom at this.

I do not have the slightest concept or ability to explain why Judge Lindsay tripled the sentence recommended by the prosecution. I have no idea why after tripling the number of days, he then changed the definition of this effort from "detention" to "incarceration." There is a significant difference between the two.

I began serving the "home incarceration" on Tuesday, May 24, 2016. Unless something changed, this sentence would be concluded on Sunday, August 21, 2016. In counting the days on a calendar, the final day of the ninety days falls on the Sunday. As I indicated elsewhere, the ninety days became three months on the official court order. What did this mean? Since the ninety-day schedule would have ended on August 21 (a Sunday), then statute allows any form of incarceration to conclude on the Friday preceding. My final day was going to be Friday, August 19. Since the order stated "three months," the date for termination of the incarceration became Tuesday, 23 August. This one change effectively added four days to my sentence.

I paid the fine, the $25 court clerk fee, and the restitution ordered before leaving the courthouse. Should the other individual not make any payments of his half of the restitution, it would immediately fall to me to pay anyway. I chose not to belabor the point and paid the entire restitution. When I asked how I might get my part of this money reimbursed, the probation officer in Louisville told me I could take Mr. Miller to court. You can imagine my feelings about this response.

During his closing, Magistrate Judge Lindsay stated he had considered my previous service to my country, that I had no previous charges of any kind, and all the letters written on my behalf. He indicated there was no need for the federal probation officers to conduct any drug screening, as there were no instances of drug abuse indicated. Judge Lindsay then said that my sentence was as lenient as it was only because of my record and the many letters. He felt that I had not indicated or shown any remorse for my actions, and he felt the sentence was required. I found this to be incredible! My offense was an offense of omission. I was charged with failure to report. To imply that I should be remorseful for not reporting something I was never informed was required, knowing that my inaction was based on the report of a trusted and experienced investigator who had told me that "contact, if contact occurred, was in her view accidental" caused my blood pressure to rise! His actions at the conclusion of this case seemed to shout, "I know something you don't know about this case, and I have the power to correct a great wrong." I only hope at some future date, Magistrate Judge Lindsay has the opportunity to know the truth and lament his pronouncement.

10

COMPLETING THE SENTENCE

Man is guaranteed only those rights which he can
defend.

—Jack McCoy

Fiat Justitia ruat caelum. Let Justice be done
though the heavens fall.

—Lucius Calpurnius Piso Caesoninus

I returned home on Thursday afternoon after the sentence was delivered in the courtroom. I had paid the fine, the court costs, and the
restitution identified. My only remaining activity was to complete
the ninety days (three months) of home incarceration ordered by
Magistrate Judge Lindsay. The ninety days expressed in court was
changed to read "three months" on the signed order. This one change,
coupled with the date my actual home incarceration began, effectively
added four days to my sentence. We stopped in Elizabethtown and
had lunch with the church members who had driven to Louisville for
this sentencing hearing. I had hoped their presence and the ninety

letters of character support would be considered during the pronouncement of the sentence.

After arriving home, I loaded my lawn mower and proceeded to mow my mother's yard, the yard of a lady from our church, and the Lions Club property lawn. I completed these and got home, hoping to mow my yard one additional time before the sentence was imposed. While mowing my yard, an idler pulley on the mower broke. I was unable to complete this task. My brother came by to express his dismay at the sentence. Upon hearing about my situation, he drove home, picked up his mower, and returned to mow my yard. Over the next day or two, no less than five people offered to mow my yard over the period of the sentencing. Another Lions Club member stepped up to mow that yard. Another church member indicated he would mow the ladies yard I had been mowing. God, in His infinite wisdom, presents solutions to all problems.

I had been dismayed at Magistrate Judge Lindsay's refusal to allow me to attend church, teach my Sunday school Class, perform my deacon duties, or perform my business meeting moderator duties. At the conclusion of the sentencing, I told some of my Sunday school members that I guessed we would have to conduct Sunday school at my house. This concept took fire, and we conducted the class at our home every Sunday. Sunday is the only day of the week that I was in what is called "lockdown" status. Monday through Saturday, I was allowed to travel from home to my mother's home to assist in her caregiving. This window granted by the probation office was from 5:30 to 10:00 a.m., from the time I could leave until the time I must be home. Only in emergency situations could this schedule be altered.

The federal probation office was very fair and courteous during my every contact with them, whether in Louisville or at my home. All of them were very professional and considerate in their duties. This aspect of the entire ordeal was expected to be the worst aspect, and it was the best. I thank the entire organization for this courtesy and professionalism.

I could have as many visitors as desired to come during my confinement. This is why Sunday school at home was able to work.

Sheriff Gaines visited my home early in the process and wanted to escort me to the Lions Club meetings. He asked for my probation officer's name and number. He called in my presence and in the presence of my church pastor, Brother Jeff Carlisle, who was also visiting. My probation officer checked but could not allow this, based upon Magistrate Judge Lindsay's comments, but he indicated my attorney could file a motion accordingly. I think the probation office in Louisville wondered what I was doing, apparently enlisting people to call on my behalf. I later worried about this and contacted my probation officer to explain that I had asked the sheriff not to call. I explained that I offered to host the Lions Club meetings in my home, just like our Sunday school classes. I was again happy to have had understanding people in the probation office.

I chose not to expend additional future time and resources pursuing an appeal in this case. Appeals in federal court are rarely successful. My attorney is a trial attorney, and he does not do appeals, though he indicated he could refer me to some great appeal attorneys. As I considered the appeal, I found several things worth considering:

- Magistrate Judge Lindsay could not consider any appeal action, as this exceeds the authority of a magistrate judge.
- Judge McKinley, though the senior judge within the Western District of Kentucky, would probably have to recuse himself since he ruled on the original motion by denying the inclusion of the 42 USC 13031 elements.
- This potential left it up in the air as to who, within the Western District of Kentucky, might even consider and rule on an appeal. Were it a justice subordinate to Judge McKinley, could they be counted upon to rightly overrule the initial ruling?
- Were the case considered fraught with errors; would it simply be dismissed or sent back for retrial?

After considering all this and that my home incarceration would continue throughout this process, I determined not to appeal the action. This effectively ended the options regarding this particular case. Does this mean there are no other options?

There seems to have been many, many inconsistent and potentially illegal processes included in this case. I think there may be some future options to pursue remedy under one of the following; a Mandamus action (28 USC § 1361), an Administrative Procedure Act (5 USC § 701) violation, or even a Tucker Act violation. I think I can pursue any of the above actions in any federal court of my choosing, and there are liberal time standards on such filings.

Whether the Department of Justice responds favorably regarding my final request for remedy relating to the AAG Virginia Seitz opinion has little impact on potential future action. If they respond favorably, I am hopeful they choose to implement remedy under one of the available statutes available. If they choose not to act, then I have the ability to act under those same statutes at a future time and place of my choosing (within six years). Some of the other statutes allowing this include 28 USC § 1391 (e), 28 USC § 2401 (a), 28 USC § 1331, 28 USC § 2201, 5 USC § 702 and 5 USC § 704. As I indicated, I am hopeful the Department of Justice recognizes the injustice in this case and moves to remedy the situation.

The hours and minutes during the home incarceration period provided plenty of time for me to continue to write this book, research, and document my reference material and to consider how to share my side of this story. I am grateful for what technology has provided in my home. I continued to study God's Word and prepare for our weekly Sunday school lessons. The recent circumstances provided the opportunity for many added and diverse Scripture connections. I hope my class enjoyed our home classes as much as I did, and I thank both God and the members for allowing me to remain involved in this manner.

In Exodus, Scripture relates that God, through Moses, provided plagues over and over that caused much suffering in Egypt. Several times Pharaoh consented to allow Moses and the children of Israel leave, only to change his mind because God had "hardened his heart." I was teaching this scripture to my class while awaiting the sentence. I have prepared myself that God has a purpose in this effort, as it seems that Magistrate Judge Lindsay's heart was indeed hardened against all logic. I can only wait and pray to see God's plan revealed at some future date.

SECTION III

Implications
for Justice

11

LADY JUSTICE, MISDIRECTED SYMBOLISM

> The law does not expect a man to be prepared
> to defend every act of his life which may be sud-
> denly and without notice alleged against him.
>
> —John Marshall

I was just getting ready to depart the community center at the Edmonson County courthouse on Friday evening, September 26, 2014, after an evening of campaigning, when I noticed I had missed a call from Ms. Kemmye Graves. Ms. Graves had left a cryptic message to the effect that she and others had been informed they would be placed on administrative leave with pay and that she felt I would understand the meaning of this. I had heard nothing officially of the investigation or grand jury since my release from the jury room at 4:15 on March 4. Six months and twenty days had passed without any indication of an indictment or no true bill finding against my former employee, the lone alleged perpetrator in the case. My assumption had been that due to the time involved, the case apparently did not merit trial, so this new development was very troubling.

When I got home that evening, I called my former supervisor and asked if he had experienced a long day. He indicated he had. I indicated that I hoped I was not the reason for that. I asked if he could share what he knew. He indicated he was directed not to call me, but since I had called him, he would tell me what he knew. He shared that there was information that the United States district attorney would indict the individual cadre supervisor on a charge of forcible sexual relations with someone he was responsible for, a charge for attempting to interfere with an investigation, a different charge of sexual abuse against two different girls, and that five other staff and I would be charged with failure to report child abuse. I found any discussion of indictment outside the primary incident incredulous, as I knew about every instance and investigation that had happened and there was no other unreported incident of child abuse at the academy. He advised that I should wait until I receive my indictment, since something may have been represented in error.

We waited through the entire weekend to hear something from an indictment and heard nothing. On Sunday, after church, a friend campaigning for magistrate called me and asked if something was going on. I said, "Why do you ask?" He indicated he had stopped by a home in Oakland, Kentucky, to ask for the occupant's vote. They had talked about his platform, and then the occupant had asked what he knew about me. My friend indicated we had grown up together and that he knew of no person of better character in Warren County. The occupant then informed him that he had heard that some information that might reflect otherwise and that it would hit the media on Monday. I shared with my friend what I had been told, but that I had not been indicted, as far as I knew.

This family in Oakland, Kentucky, had apparently gotten their information from a very accurate source, since the indictments did make the media news on Monday evening. I received many calls that day from people who were angry about this October Surprise, and from one who asked if I had obtained counsel. I indicated that I had done nothing wrong and knew of no reason I should need counsel.

He shared that in a matter like this, counsel was the first thing I needed. He provided the name of a friend in the public defender's office in Louisville, whom he indicated would be able to recommend a qualified attorney to represent me. I called and was provided the name of Mr. Darren Wolff, a very qualified Louisville attorney and a former Marine Corps JAG Officer. Mr. Wolff has been a very understanding and knowledgeable resource during the entire ordeal.

On Monday, the indictment actually made the news in Louisville, and by Tuesday, it made the news in Bowling Green, Kentucky. I kept waiting for someone to appear at my door with an indictment. No one came. I kept waiting for a piece of registered mail that would contain the indictment, and none came. I was being asked to respond to the indictment by the media, having never received an indictment. I shared this with my attorney, and he obtained a copy of my indictment for me through the courts. My first correspondence from the United States District Court was not an indictment but a letter instructing me to contact an administrative technician for a pre-arraignment interview. The document from the administrative technician had been mailed to John E. Smith, at my physical address and not my mailing address. I was very lucky that the local post office recognized me as the intended recipient and placed the envelope in my post office box anyway.

We have a time-honored tradition in the United States military—to never leave any soldier behind, unless getting this soldier out would cost more soldiers' lives. As General Hal Moore related in his poignant book, *We Were Soldiers Once and Young*, discussing a young lieutenant who was killed when he went back to retrieve a fellow soldier; General Moore said, "He died keeping my promise." This is the spirit of leadership that has made our military esprit de corps an enviable camaraderie. Soldiers and most civil servants work very hard to carry out the lawful orders of their country, state, and their superiors every day. All those state government contract employees who were later charged with the misdemeanor charge were doing everything exactly as we had been trained. We had corrected every minor infraction identified by multiple annual inspections and attended training at every opportunity to upgrade our skills; whether for the national effort or the Commonwealth.

Once an allegation was leveled by the Office of the United States Attorney, every organization that had demanded and required the prompt attendance at training, had inspected the operations and functioning of the organization, and had considered and approved laudatory recognitions of many of those indicted turned their backs on their loyal employees. These employees were abandoned, whether they were currently employed, retired, or otherwise absent from the program they had worked so hard to improve. Legal representation existed at the Department of Military Affairs in Kentucky, the Office of the Kentucky Attorney General, and the National Guard Bureau in Arlington, Virginia, yet no one came forward to even examine what efforts had been accomplished toward the expected performance of required duties. We also see this occur on a world scale too often. While none of these personnel gave their lives in the performance of their duties; they were abandoned in much the same manner as some of our contract heroes in combat. No federal or state employee should be treated in such a manner.

I will work to accomplish at least one of the following future outcomes toward insuring this never occurs again within the Youth ChalleNGe programs, through one of the following policy changes:

- Require, through the Master Youth Program Cooperative Agreement between the states and the National Guard Bureau, a joint expectation that employees performing their duties as defined in position descriptions, through individual training and through expressed policy, will be represented by appropriate legal representation of agencies involved in the contract. Whether this representation is from the state, the federal government, or a combination of both, it must be a part of the contract.

- Federal or state law must provide direct representation of employees working to implement contractual provisions or provide a contractual option for this representation. Any contract issued by the federal government to an organization that performs compliance inspections of other governmental elements should include a clause that requires that contractor to represent any programs operating under the contract and subject to these compliance reviews. A contractor qualified to perform compliance reviews is in a better position than anyone else to determine the overall compliance. This concept is much like the bonding process any legal deed holder obtains through a title opinion search.

• Finally, assuming neither option above can be accomplished; there should be some provision for each program to place on retainer legal representation for the organization. This legal representative would consider all contractual requirements and the results of compliance reviews to identify and respond to any accusations of inappropriate response.

I firmly believe that there must be an expectation of support for every employee, former or current, who may be indicted based upon something alleged to have happened during their service to the organization. The salaries paid are insufficient for the unidentified risks associated with performing your job as you have been trained and then being accused of something you were completely unaware was a requirement or expectation.

12

FEDERAL JUSTICE
GONE ASKEW

I wished to live without committing any fault at any time; I would conquer all that either natural inclination, custom, or company might lead me into. As I knew, or thought I knew, what was right and wrong, I did not see why I might not always do the one and avoid the other. But I soon found I had undertaken a task of more difficulty than I had imagined. While my care was employed in guarding against one fault, I was often surprised by another.

—Benjamin Franklin

My primary involvement with law enforcement has previously been to assist in the development of cases, either as a volunteer firefighter and former chief of the Smiths Grove rural fire department or as chief of staff of the Kentucky National Guard. Serving as a juror or as a witness relating to first responder duties are the only judicial encounters my wife, our four children, or I have been involved in prior to this. I have now learned what it means to be on the receiving end of a misguided indictment. I fully believed that our system of checks and balances in government was at least as strong in our judicial system, if not stronger. I believed that government developed a case using the "whole truth and nothing but the truth." I am no longer as naïve as I once was.

I have learned the power of the prosecutor resembles an unchecked dynamo or runaway train in our system of justice. I have studied many articles in the past year that call for a complete revamp of our grand jury system to create a more people-centric view of prosecution. How strange it seemed to learn that the idea of the British grand jury, an idea continued in colonial America, was to be an unquestionable gate to limit the unjust prosecution of individuals by the government. The current role and position of the grand jury seems completely at odds with that concept. The grand jury has become the unquestionable arm of the prosecution to insure the indictment of any person or persons the prosecutor wants to charge.

While much is written concerning justice and injustice within our system and often debated among legal scholars, few changes trickle down to our courts. Politicians and prosecutors scream for justice. Victims' rights, or the expressed exclusion of the same, are used to prescribe new laws. Child abuse had become one of the politically correct and unquestionable charges against citizens, teachers, schools, and even churches. There is an automatic presumption of guilt that follows the announced crime. Whether it involves politically correct, politically motivated, or even politically safe allegations, there are some things about our system of justice everyone should know.

If questioned by the FBI, you should always make sure you have an attorney present. I was a retired Youth ChalleNGe program director, two months removed from any Academy records. I was six months removed from any knowledge of the August 9, 2013 incident that had been immediately reported to the Fort Knox CID. I was one year removed from the sexual harassment investigation that resulted in the visit to my home by the FBI. I did not have to welcome the FBI into my home on short notice. I should have asked for a description of what they needed to know and advised them that my attorney and I would meet them at the attorney's office.

When I received the subpoena to testify before the grand jury, I again expected that I was there to answer any questions the grand jury might have. My only involvement in the August 9, 2013 incident investigation, as it was immediately referred to the CID, was providing any support asked of me by the CID and FBI in a very timely manner until I retired. I tried to respond to requests for information or documents on the same day if at all possible. A person appearing before the grand jury may have an attorney outside the witness room; however, that person must ask to leave to ask for advice. The attorney cannot accompany the witness in the room. This is the only situation in American justice where a person is denied legal representation during questioning.

The Department of Justice rules suggest that a potential target of an indictment be so notified of this when they appear before a grand jury. It is not required, and neither I nor any of my other staff that appeared before the grand jury were advised of this status. In differentiating between the duties and responsibilities of the grand jury versus those of a petit (trial) jury, here are a few that I have learned:

The prosecutor is not required to present any exculpatory evidence to the grand jury. This means any evidence showing that the target of the indictment is probably innocent in not required to be shared. In our circumstances, none of the previous times we had reached out to the CID or military police were shared. Neither the number of the other sexual harassment investigations Ms. Graves conducted on site during her ten-plus years in this role, nor were the number of times she had been used by the Commonwealth of Kentucky outside the Youth ChalleNGe program shared. Rather, it was consistently presented to the grand jury that she was not a trained criminal investigator. That all national Youth ChalleNGe programs are Title IX entities (Title IX became federal law as a portion of the federal Education Amendments of 1972; specifically, Public Law No. 92-318, 86 Stat. 235 (June 23, 1972), and codified at 20 U.S.C. § 1681–1688.), just like all schools and universities. This status, by constitutional law, requires all sexual harassment allegations to be investigated was never mentioned. It was never mentioned that the Fort Knox representative of the Attorney General had failed to meet any of the required responsibilities under 42 USC § 13031[3] relating to Bluegrass ChalleNGe Academy.

The prosecutor may use hearsay evidence in the grand jury proceeding. This same evidence will not be allowed to be presented in a normal trial.

The prosecutor may be very theatrical in making his presentation to the grand jury in order to convince the grand jury that something has occurred. At one time, CPT Turner asked if I had any daughters. When I replied in the affirmative, he stood up, grasped his right hand with his left hand, and simulated pulling his right hand to his crotch and grinding it there. He then asked if I would recognize this action as sexual abuse. I replied that I would. While this action was nothing near what had been briefed to me at the time of the February 8, 2013 sexual harassment investigation; this affirmative response on my part was to be used as an indication that I was aware of that sexual abuse had occurred and had failed to report it. Only CPT Turner, those present, and I will ever know that this occurred in the grand jury proceeding. Nothing on the transcript (which is also not available for public review) of the interview indicated the theatrics of the moment. I credit Magistrate Judge Lindsay with a correct ruling when he refused to allow any of the testimony regarding my daughters to be read into the record during the trial. He recognized it for what it was and sternly admonished any idea that it would be asked to be allowed. My point here is this: if something is so perverse that the judge reacts to it in such a manner in chambers, how can it be allowed to occur in a grand jury presentation?

- In our testimony before the grand jury, we each expected the line of questioning regarding the case we each thought we were there to testify regarding to be the August 9, 2013 incident. If substantiated, this allegation would clearly be child abuse, and it was immediately reported by the

---

3   . https://www.law.cornell.edu/uscode/text/42/13031

academy. This incident was constantly mixed during the grand jury questioning with the previous investigation of alleged sexual harassment. It seemed the Prosecutor tried to blur the two cases, and by doing so, he implied that all those involved in the earlier investigation had caused the second incident to happen.

- The grand jury proceedings are secret. No transcript of the discussions that occur between the grand jury members or by the prosecutor to the grand jurors can be made public. Witness transcripts are a part of the record, if presented in trial proceedings, and then only through direct examination of that witness or having approved elements of the defendant's testimony read by someone else. Nothing said by the prosecutor to the grand jurors or by the grand jurors to the prosecutor will ever be known outside that room. Only through complacent interjections by the prosecutor during other witness interviews was I able to see how much influence the prosecutor exerted on the grand jury through their expressed and unwarranted opinion of what had happened.

- The prosecutor determines the charge relating to the indictment. Further, the power of the prosecutor goes far beyond that. Here are some of the instances:

    - The prosecutor decides beforehand if the allegation is worthy of consideration by the state or the grand jury. Their justification not to pursue indictment cannot be questioned, regardless of the amount of physical evidence indicating that the indictment is warranted.

    - The prosecutor can also choose to bring before the grand jury a charge that is completely without merit. The grand juror is the only check in the system to prevent an innocent person from being charged. There are two widely held sentiments by prosecutors regarding grand jury efforts: one indicates that any prosecutor is able to indict a ham sandwich in most grand jury proceedings, and another indicates, "Show me the person, and I will find the crime." The prosecutor is generally not personally liable for these types of frivolous indictments, and the ability of the defendant to be awarded a judgment for legal expenses is virtually nonexistent.

- The prosecutor typically tends to overcharge the individual in an indictment. This allows for pretrial negotiations to create a plea agreement to a lesser charge or to a pretrial diversion. Both are much less than the grand jurors expected, but either result in a win for the prosecutor.

- The prosecutor, after the grand jury indictment, can change the charge completely or even dismiss the charge before going to court. Again, none of these actions require any disclosure on the part of the prosecutor as to reasons.

Many legal scholars have written about the modern grand jury proceedings. Many suggestions have been offered to move the grand jury back to its intended place as a wall between unnecessary prosecutions by the state against the innocent or unaware citizen. Remember, this was the basis for a secret and without review process in the British legal system grand jury, to protect the accused and the grand jury from the state. Here are some of the widely recommended changes that would move the proceedings in the right direction:

- Require the same evidentiary rules in the grand jury as the petit jury. If evidence is not allowed to be presented in the trial, it should not be allowed to be presented to the grand jury.

- Require all targets of potential indictment to be so notified. If a witness to the grand jury is not a target, then provide a pre-testimony document to them stating that they are not a target and no indictment will be forthcoming as a result of this testimony. It is also the policy of the

United States Department of Justice that targets of prosecution be so notified, though this policy is apparently often disregarded.

- Allow witnesses before the grand jury to have legal representation present during testimony. This would just bring the grand jury in legal compliance with every other legal proceeding from police questioning to final trial.

- Eliminate plea bargaining and pretrial diversion from the legal tool bag. If the grand jury indicts on a specific charge or crime; that charge should then be the charge of record that will either result in a plea of guilty, consideration in an appropriate trial, or being dismissed by the prosecution. This one outcome would result in the elimination of many unnecessary trials. If prosecutors were held to conducting a trial under all the legal conventions and not able to change the charges under a plea agreement; then more justice would be accomplished.

- Advise the grand jury of their historic role in the legal process. They must know that their role is to prevent the unwarranted indictment of anyone without probable cause. They must have all the evidence and not just what the prosecutor wants to share regarding potential guilt of the accused. All too often, the grand jury believes it is their responsibility to assist the prosecution in bringing the accused to trial. After all, each defendant will then have their chance in court. This is not what our founders envisioned. After being duly advised of this responsibility, provide that the grand jury be required to report any comments or activities by the prosecutor during the presentation that caused concern of any of the members.

- Create a rule that requires the prosecution to be responsible for the defendant's court and defense costs when indicted individuals are found not guilty. While this provision is included in Title 42 United States Code, § 13031 (f), allowing the defendant to sue for this in these cases, it is very difficult to prove. Surely, the prosecution's

argument would be that "we must take every allegation
of child abuse seriously and prosecute to the maximum."
Changing the rule to include all instances of "not guilty"
verdicts should eliminate the overreach of overzealous
Prosecutors.

As we consider these changes to our grand jury system, we
must consider the implications to our criminal justice system as well.
These changes portend a new view of criminal justice in America.
Is it a change to create the expectation that everyone has the right
of the presumption of innocence until proven guilty in a court of
law? With this presumption, how can anyone agreeing to a pretrial
diversion ever be considered guilty? How can the pretrial diversion
document state both the presumption of guilt while acknowledging
that all charges will dismissed after the period listed and never be
brought up again? With a presumption of innocence, how could any
future employer even ask, "Have you ever accepted an Alford Plea?"
How can any plea agreement, where a defendant pleads guilty to one
or multiple lesser crimes to gain a reduced charge in a felony charge,
ever be allowed to be considered as fact that even one or any of the
lesser crimes actually occurred? This situation occurs many times in
our nation each year.

We must restore the beliefs our Founders so eloquently defined,
when quill was put to ink and then to paper, that the courts are there
to protect the citizens from the rampant expansion of a government
and the mechanisms of justice created by an expanding system. Lady
Justice should face the courthouse to defend the citizens instead of
facing outward.

What concerns do I now have relating to the current system?

- The system is designed to reward prosecutors whose
  records are inflated due to the number of convictions they
  obtain. I was told during this process that you seldom see
  a successful defense attorney appointed to a federal judge-
  ship. Of course there are multiple reasons for this, but it
  becomes painfully obvious once you consider the ladder

to success in our court system. A successful defense attorney may have no desire to accept a federal judge appointment, as it would be financially harmful. What unsuccessful prosecutor would ever be considered for a judicial appointment? As you can readily see, the system becomes a self-sustaining prosecutorial promotion system.

- Why are there so many indictments that end in pretrial diversions or plea bargain outcomes? The nature of the charges and their potential punishments, coupled with the long drawn out nature of trials and the costs of defense, force people of normal means into this outcome at some time before a case ever goes to trial. Very few have the resources or time to just wait until their case can be heard by a jury of their peers. Who benefits from this situation? The judge benefits as the case doesn't come to trial. A case that does not go to trail can never be challenged or appealed. The prosecutor benefits as the pretrial diversion or the plea agreement can be considered a win in their column at the time, even though it may be completely dismissed at a later date. The defense attorney benefits because their representation of a client has resulted in a significant fee to their firm without a single day in the courtroom. The person accepting the pretrial diversion or the plea agreement benefits from having the process conclude, having a point in time in the future when the charge may be dismissed, and they stop the bleeding of their personal finances. I hope this realization that our system of justice has developed to a point where everyone seems to benefit; however, the defendant is the only place where a significant negative redistribution of wealth occurs. Legal scholars agree that removing the pretrial diversion and plea agreement, coupled with a mechanism to force those bringing the charge to bear the burden of cost related to "not guilty" verdicts, would do more to change our judicial system than any other action.

- Are there significant crimes occurring in our country that deserve the very best effort of our criminal investigators and courts? Absolutely! Is it much safer and less stressful to investigate and try a case of minimal criminality and with a likely pretrial diversion outcome? Where do you want your law enforcement and prosecution assets efforts expended?

- Are defense attorneys going to complain about a system that causes a large number of innocent people to require representation? Would you complain about a system that insures you have a steady stream of clients, facing their first charge, and able (some through the support of family) to pay your fee, and who will only learn later that the charge will likely be reduced or dismissed if you accept a plea bargain or pretrial diversion? My attorney provided the very best effort I could have desired in the case. Not one time did he urge me to accept the diversion rather than go to trial; though he made the opportunity known to me on several occasions. I will leave it to each of the other defendants in our case to share what their attorneys presented to them.

Another part of the federal process that caused me much trepidation was the process of pre-indictment scrutiny given the resources of my family to determine whether I would be an apparent flight risk. I appeared before an administrative clerk long before I appeared before a judge, or even my attorney, to make my plea of "not guilty." During this interview, I was required to state the value of my checking account, savings account, value of my holdings in property, value of personal possessions, whether I owned a gun, whether I had dogs in my home, the names and addresses of my children and other personal information. All this to allegedly determine if a man who had received only one speeding ticket in his life, who had served his country in the military for twenty-eight years, who had served his state as the primary agent for an at-risk youth program, who had and was holding leadership positions with their church, was a risk to the government of leaving the country rather than face misdemeanor prosecution. Is this really necessary? And at the end of the administrative process, I was asked who my attorney was and informed that this information would be shared with the court and my attorney. At the end of the process, I wondered if the process was more about my ability to pay the fee or be referred to a public defender. Having this information prior to any discussions of total fee is definitely a benefit to any attorney in the fee negotiation.

United States Code requires trials to occur within a set period of time. This clock begins when an indictment occurs. In my case and everyone else indicted in the misdemeanor case, there was no notice we were targets of an indictment, or any reason to believe we would be indicted. During the initial plea appearance, all misdemeanor defendants entered a plea of "not guilty," and we were released on our own recognizance. The judge set a date for trial approximately forty-five days later. At that moment, my attorney indicated that this was just a date selected for the trial and that our actual trail date would be much later. He expected a March date to be the actual target date. As it turned out, the initial date was set for June. During the process, all the misdemeanor defendants urged that the misdemeanor case be separated from the felony case of the primary defendant. They were two very different situations, separated by six months. The judge denied the motions to separate. As we neared the June date, the prosecutor decided to supersede the charge against the primary defendant. This change of charge caused an immediate request for additional time to prepare for the new charge by his attorney on his behalf. This was a great time to cause the two cases to be separated on the judicial calendar, but all misdemeanor attorneys indicated that a delay in trial was always more beneficial to the defense than the prosecution. My attorney and I were the last to consent to an extension, even though I felt that our trying to obtain a trial on our own was futile. Soon after the new delay in the trial date, the ADA offered the pretrial diversion to the misdemeanor defendants. As indicated, four of the six accepted the initial offer. I guess the delay of the trial *was* beneficial to the ADA (got to count this as four wins), the attorneys (got significant fees and never presented any argument in court), and the defendants (stopped the constant drain on their finances and identified a date when the entire thing went away).

Later, the ADA changed the primary charge against the primary defendant to a state charge of "sodomy". This charge resulted in a plea agreement between the ADA and the primary defendant. This change, on its face, seemed to acknowledge a consensual sexual act between the student and former staff member. This contact was still wrong and deserving of punishment on his part. This new activity resulted in another meeting where the only other misdemeanor defendant decided to accept a further modified pretrial diversion, similar to the others but where the comment that she "knew or suspected" a crime had been committed was removed, and additional language was added as well. In July 2015, I became the only defendant who declined to sign a document indicating that I was aware of or suspected an act of child abuse had occurred and failed to report it. The next pretrial conference was set for October 28, 2015, with trial proceeding on November 9, 10, and 12.

Has all this caused me to view our criminal justice system in a new light? My view of the common citizen's hopes to be involved in a positive way to insure justice has not wavered. I have a new realization that the justice machine is unconcerned that innocent Americans will undergo the process, and what is worse is that the prosecution feels this condition may be necessary to insure that the system continues to operate. Until we create a reversal of the costs associated with this type prosecution, there will be no incentive to stop indicting citizens based on a premise that they "can have their day in court" mentality. I hope you become as energized as I am to see this change occur.

Does our system of justice have recourse elements to provide the common man the opportunity to achieve justice in his case? Absolutely! If there is a ruling counter to the law made by a judge and the law seems fairly clear, a Mandamus action could take place to challenge the ruling. If the jury rules against the defendant, appeal is always an option. In cases where agents of the United States have knowingly violated the rights of an individual or organization, where expressed law or opinion define the correct actions expected, the defendant has extended recourse outside appeal. Generally, there is one common denominator in all these efforts—representation. Each effort mentioned above requires some specific knowledge and skill to successfully execute. Would anyone feel it appropriate to undertake any of the above for just a misdemeanor? That has been the eternal question throughout this ordeal.

I was recently asked if I continue to state "Justice for all" when I recite the Pledge of Allegiance to the Flag. I replied that I do. I do so now as it is our national pledge of something to be aspired to, not something that is currently guaranteed. Do all our citizens know and appreciate the meaning of our Pledge of Allegiance to the Flag or our National Anthem? Simply watching any group participate in the Pledge of Allegiance or the National Anthem will provide ample proof that too few actually understand, or even appreciate, the significance of either.

13

FEDERAL RESPONSIBILITY DISREGARDED

> It will be of little avail to the people that the laws
> are made by men of their own choice if the laws
> are so voluminous that they cannot be read, or so
> incoherent that they cannot be understood.
>
> —James Madison

During my preparation for the defense of the indictment against me and others, I also found what was lacking from the government in the case. We operated Bluegrass ChalleNGe Academy (BCA) with the understanding that both the federal government (National Guard Bureau, NGB) and the state (Department of Military Affairs, DMA) expected the program to be a "state" program. Our Master Youth Program Cooperative Agreement (MYPCA) [our contract with National Guard Bureau] and our state policies dictated as much. In most conflicting issues, the MYPCA defers to the state on matters of legislative requirements and budgetary execution.

The program underwent both multi-day annual performance evaluations by agencies contracted by NGB and biennial multi-day fiscal examinations during my tenure as director. Additionally, the United States Property and Fiscal Office (USPFO) conducted audits of our efforts and follow-ups on these inspections. On at least two occasions during my tenure, BCA's inspection reports reflected "no deficiencies." A "no deficiencies" outcome is not the result of a single person's efforts. It is the result of a concerted effort of all staff members within the organization.

Having already considered the discussion of the charges against us earlier, you surely noted that the charge existed solely due to our operation of the Youth ChalleNGe Program on a military installation. The jurisdiction on a military installation or United States maritime vessel is absolute, especially when the state has ceded jurisdiction to the Fort legislatively. During my entire 10.5 years of service as director, we constantly fought to identify the agency with jurisdiction relating to the program. There is a memorandum of agreement between the provost marshal of Fort Knox, the sheriff of Hardin County, and judges of the Hardin District Court on the subject. This document specifies how the jurisdiction involving investigation and potential criminal charges will be addressed. My new appreciation of the federal legal statutes and the state statute ceding jurisdiction to Fort Knox has caused a new realization that there should be no need for a memorandum of agreement as Fort Knox has complete jurisdictional authority. Additionally, while the entire purpose of this memorandum regards Bluegrass ChalleNGe Academy, no person representing the Academy or the Department of Military Affairs was indicated as participating during the drafting and completion of the document. The academy did not receive a copy of this document from any of the signatories on the agreement. I received a copy of the document from a local Court Designated Worker (CDW) a year or more after it was signed.

As we were charged under Title 18 United States Code § 2258 – Failure to Report Child Abuse[4], I felt as victimized as those I had

---

[4]   https://www.law.cornell.edu/uscode/text/18/2258

tried to protect. I wondered why no one at NGB or DMA had ever shared these very serious possibilities or responsibilities. The obvious answer is that both organizations thought that the program, also established by United States Code, was a state program. I wondered how someone could be charged under a statute they had no knowledge even existed.

Title 18 USC § 2258 is the citation for a violation of 42 USC § 13031. As you can see in paragraphs (d), (e), (f) and (h) of 42 USC § 13031, the Attorney General has clearly defined responsibilities to notify all identified personnel of their specific responsibilities, to designate the agency to report such suspect events to for investigation, to provide the reporting format for such reports and to provide periodic training. None of this was provided by any representative of the attorney general or of Fort Knox to Bluegrass ChalleNGe Academy or to the Department of Military Affairs, to my knowledge. I have no knowledge of how the Attorney General or Fort Knox deals with their traditional schools on this subject. I do suspect BCA is, and was, the largest organization on Fort Knox housing sixteen- to eighteen-year-old youth as a residential facility. Expectations are that BCA would be at the top of everyone's list to insure all the requirements of Title 42 United States Code § 13031 were met.

Additionally, our fiscal and organizational posture was dictated through the annual budgetary process of the federal government and the biennial Kentucky state budget process. During my ten-year tenure as director, we were constantly attempting to do more with lesser funds. Our manning authorizations were defined by our national contract. Minimum and maximum staffing limits were specified for each staff position. As you can imagine, if anyone identified an outside agency to conduct all suspected child abuse investigations, which would have to be extended to sexual harassment allegations due to our indictment; it does not take long to consider or implement that process. The program would be absolved of cost, manpower, and legal responsibility in the outcome of any and all investigations. To call this a no-brainer is not a stretch in any rational person's mind.

During the entire period of the indictment of my former staff under Title 18, I wondered how the government, and especially a military law captain serving as the special assistant district attorney for Fort Knox would not invoke paragraph (f) for all my subordinate staff members. The program, both in national contract, state policy and even certain memorandum of agreement, identifies a military chain of command for all reporting. The aforementioned memorandum of agreement between Fort Knox and the Department of Military Affairs requires the director to report any suspected legal violations. Staff members who were involved at all levels in the reporting, request for investigation, investigation, and execution of recommendations stemming from the investigation should never be considered for indictment. All these staff members did their full duty in reporting the situation up the chain of command and took appropriate actions relating to a reported instance of alleged sexual harassment. The Academy EEOC representative conducted a timely and comprehensive investigation, expressing her conclusions and identifying processes to preclude these allegations from occurring again. Had they been followed, no future allegation would occur. If the special assistant district attorney for Fort Knox felt there was any responsibility in the outcome of the investigation, it should rest solely with the director of the program. At this juncture, I remain steadfast in my belief that everything done in the case was done correctly, the investigation was conducted in an appropriate manner, and the recommendations for closure were appropriate.

I have written both NGB and DMA to advise them that there should be a complete review of jurisdictional issues regarding any Youth ChalleNGe program located on a military installation. Each program should contact their local Judge Advocate General (JAG) office and request appropriate information and training in accordance with the requirements of Title 42 United States Code § 13031. I prepared a briefing for current Kentucky Youth ChalleNGe Directors, the staff they brought to the presentation, to the Executive Director, Office of Management and Administration, Department of Military Affairs, his assistant and the departmental legal advisor regarding the same in early 2016. My aim was to share that the requirements of Title IX sexual harassment investigations and the requirements of 42 USC § 13031 cannot be considered separate efforts. Ignoring the Title IX requirement places programs at risk of losing the 75 percent federal funding. Ignoring the 42 USC § 13031 reporting requirements places staff in the same position for indictment as we experienced. I recommended that all allegations of sexual harassment be both investigated and reported. In this manner all potential negative outcomes are addressed. This effort, meant as a positive effort, was later held against me (to be described later).

Additionally, through my exhaustive efforts to come to some official resolutions in this matter, I later learned of the Department of Justice, Office of Legal Counsel (OLC) Published Opinion regarding 42 USC § 13031.[5] This opinion was written by Assistant Attorney General Virginia Seitz, coordinated among the executive agencies, and published in May 2012. These published OLC opinions have "force of law" status for all executive agencies. A complete text of the opinion is included as an appendix to this journal. In this opinion, Ms. Seitz indicates that not every covered professional should be charged with failure to report. At a minimum, she indicates that the required reporting format must be provided to these covered professionals. She goes on to indicate that Congress also intended that periodic training must be provided. I will discuss Ms. Seitz's opinion more in the trial portion of this recounting.

---

[5] https://www.justice.gov/sites/default/files/olc/opinions/2012/05/31/aag-reporting-abuse.pdf

14

TITLE IX VERSUS 18 USC § 2258

Justice denied anywhere diminishes justice everywhere

—Martin Luther King, Jr.

As already stated, the United States Attorney chose to seek the indictment of the primary defendant in case in the case involving Jane Doe #1 and indict six other individuals in this case for failure to report child abuse. This action was based on the review of a staff-initiated sexual harassment allegation by a cadet.

The national Youth ChalleNGe program is required to implement the provisions of Title IX as part of our operational structure. The Master Youth Program Cooperative Agreement (MYPCA) directs this in an unequivocal manner. Many view Title IX as that federal program that impacts sports programs in schools, requiring an equal number of male and female sports programs. Title IX goes far beyond this simple connotation.

Title IX is the federal program, rather federal law as a portion of the federal Education Amendments of 1972; specifically, Public Law No. 92-318, 86 Stat. 235 (June 23, 1972), and codified at 20 U.S.C. § 1681–1688, that requires any organization receiving funding for education to insure there is no sexual discrimination within the organization. This includes all facets of sexual harassment, i.e. student-on-student, staff-on-student, instructor-on-student, and student-on-staff/instructor. Title IX has a very specific set of guidelines for these organizations, universities, colleges, local schools, military schools, local government schools—*any* organization receiving federal dollars for education, to follow.

The primary agency for the implementation of Title IX is the United States Department of Education. There is a long list of executive agencies that are also responsible under the Department of Education to both implement and enforce Title IX within their agencies. In the case of the National Guard Youth ChalleNGe Program the Executive Agency is the Department of Defense. Responsible agents under the Department of Defense include the National Guard Bureau, Office of Athletics and Youth Programs and the various states contractually obligated under the MYPCA.

The enforcement agency for Title IX issues lies within the United States Department of Education, Office of Civil Rights (DOE/OCR). This office often conducts Compliance Reviews to insure that key operational elements are being correctly implemented and addressed. Many of the high profile university and college sexual harassment scandals have resulted in DOE/OCR compliance reviews and identified processes and procedures that need correction. Many of these cases are well known to most readers and do not require restating. If you conduct an internet search referencing Title IX Compliance Reviews or Title IX Sexual Harassment Investigations, you will find a wealth of information regarding responsibilities and expectations relating to schools and administrators.

Many of the cases involving university, college, and local school board actions have resulted in civil actions for damages to alleged victims and their education. The United States Supreme Court has held that the claimant may seek damages from a respondent (the alleged harasser) in all cases where harassment or abuse occurred. The Supreme Court has limited any civil action against universities, colleges, school boards, school administrators, Title IX coordinators and other staff to those instances where there is an egregious and conscious effort by the organization to cover up or minimize the situation presented. Case intricacy and history in these instances are shared in the following Supreme Court Cases: *Jackson v. Birmingham Board of Education, Davis v. Monroe County Board of Education, 526 U.S. 629 (1999), or Franklin v. Gwinnett County Public Schools*, 503 U.S. 60 (1992). You will find the issue of Title IX sexual harassment a much argued and well-opined subject. You will find that in all cases, schools that quickly and completed investigated cases, arrive at solutions to eliminate any future harassment, do not affect the claimant's ability to participate or successfully complete the program of education, and prohibit any retaliation related to the incident in question enjoy the full support of the courts upholding their efforts.

Where the organization met and followed Title IX guidelines to the best of its ability and knowledge, all parties other than the alleged harasser are held harmless from civil liability. This preemption of state law by Title IX is formalized in many instances, including those listed above.

In our standard of law and due process in America, law is law, and the standards for case development are the same. In all cases of judicial undertaking, federal law preempts state law. Most of the historic cases you read about or watch unfold on the nightly news involve state universities, colleges, or school boards, persons in school or the state government situations usually file suit, or are charged, in state courts. Title IX is automatically invoked as it always preempts the state charge.

In the Bluegrass ChalleNGe Academy indictment, the charges are federal. This is not by any special or extra-evil wrongdoing; rather, it is due to the physical location of the academy. As the Bluegrass ChalleNGe Academy is located on the Fort Knox Army Installation, then the federal law that applies to all federal lands applies. Unfortunately, I have not found any instance regarding Title IX preempting any other federal law. Generally, it is not felt that any one federal law can preempt any other federal law, though the Civil Rights Act and Fourteenth Amendment opinions can overrule convictions in other federal laws.

After much review of the existing case opinions, I am convinced that Title IX preempts all other federal law in the instance of a sexual harassment investigation within any covered agency, regardless of location. Since multiple opinions state that Title IX preempts civil law in all instances for organizations, administrators, and supervisory personnel then the same preemption must be applied in the case of criminal law in like cases. My premise is not that organizations and individuals are automatically and expressly immune from prosecution. My premise is that there must be a DOE/OCR compliance review of the situation to determine if, in the views of Title IX procedures and expectations, a crime or crimes based on the outcomes of a Title IX sexual harassment investigation were committed. At the point the compliance review indicates this is the case, then the organization, the administrators, and the staff involved would be subject to criminal prosecution, or civil liability, depending upon the opinions of the prosecutors and/or grand jury. At this point, the Department of Education, Office of Civil Rights would have one additional consideration—either to withdraw any federal funding from the entity or to establish additional procedures to insure no further oversight. Any other conclusion seems to contravene existing Supreme Court thought and opinion.

Processes for Title IX considerations are spelled out in the document at http://knowyourix.org/title-ix/title-ix-in-detail. The Bluegrass ChalleNGe Academy standing operating procedures were adapted from the Commonwealth of Kentucky, Department of Military Affairs guidelines that incorporate or exceed all the standards listed above. Kentucky departments, and some universities, expressly utilize the Equal Employment Opportunity Commission (EEOC) representatives as the Title IX Coordinator. This usage is accepted within many national Title IX organizations.

In the current case:

- The allegation was staff-initiated rather than student-initiated. Upon hearing a report by a different cadet, the platoon teacher notified a supervisor who was not the subject of the allegation, and they conducted a preliminary investigation of comments made.

- Upon hearing comments that could be interpreted as sexual harassment, the supervisor took the notes to the commandant of the program, who supervised all aspects of cadet life in the academy. The commandant immediately formally requested the academy EEOC representative to conduct an investigation of the allegations.

- The academy EEOC representative began the investigation the next day and completed the investigation within five days of the allegations being made known. The Title IX standard maximum number of allowed days is sixty.

- The academy EEOC utilized cadet interviews (taped), staff interviews (named individual taped), review of security video, and review of site and situation evidence.

- The academy EEOC representative had no evidence of any previous complaint against the named supervisor. The action that resulted in alleged contact was requested by the cadet. The supervisor responded to the request in an immediate fashion, involving a female staff member to assist. The female staff member was present and viewing the uniform accessory installation during a period of time just before the cadet departed the office. The doors to the office were open. Other female cadets were walking up and down the hallway outside the open door during the time of the accessory installation.

- The academy EEOC representative, based on consideration of all evidence, verbally indicated that she felt that any contact, if contact occurred, was accidental and in performance of his duties.

- The academy EEOC representative, in an effort to insure that no such future allegations occur, reiterated academy guidance relating to the "three-foot rule" and the "no touch

Rule" by also advising male supervisor to utilize available female cadre to make requested uniform adjustments.
- All parties signed the report of the investigation.
- The program director reviewed the report with all parties present, getting concurrence that all parties agreed with the recommendations, that they had signed the report as an expression of their agreement, that all knew of their right to appeal the investigation to Frankfort at any time, and reinforcing that all knew that he would act immediately if any reported retaliation occurred.

Title IX also required organizations to insure that any incident and the outcome of any investigation not prohibit the student from a quality education opportunity. The cadets involved in the staff-initiated claim graduated from the program at the highest level of rank within the program. During later months, Jane Doe #1 played softball for the academy team, with the supervisor as coach. During a final pre-graduation self-assessment, Jane Doe #1 identified the supervisor as the "staff or cadre having the most positive impact" during her stay at the academy. There were no other sexual harassment allegations or complaints against the supervisor by anyone during this class period.

As I became aware of the Supreme Courts view of Title IX, I submitted an e-mail request to the Department Of Education/ Office of Civil Rights (DOE/OCR) for a compliance review of this Bluegrass ChalleNGe Academy investigation. While I did not expect DOE/OCR to conduct the investigation, I did expect that they would direct the appropriate executive agency agent (DOD or NGB) to conduct the investigation. I waited a month and then resubmitted my e-mail request, adding the constituent assistance e-mail address of Congressman Brett Guthrie in the courtesy copy line. A later meeting with the Congressman may have resulted in a Philadelphia representative of the DOE/OCR calling.

Did I expect Congressman Guthrie to personally intervene in my legal case? No! I did hope that he would contact the DOE/OCR to share his concerns for any other agency placed in the same position I and my staff have been placed. If, after conducting a compliance review the organization is found without fault, then the broader concept of law will need to be addressed. As the DOE/OCR and the Department of Justice, Office of Civil Rights (DOJ/OCR) work hand in hand on this issue, I was hopeful that a new view of the investigation can be adopted by DOJ. There must be criminal guidance as well as the Supreme Court civil guidance. Until there is a test case, none of this can be addressed.

I was later contacted by a representative of the Department of Education, Office of Civil Rights office in Philadelphia, telephonically. As with all calls of this nature the gentleman spoke quickly and without a chance to record the name. He indicated that the DOE, OCR only conducted compliance reviews regarding DOE-funded schools. He had researched Bluegrass ChalleNGe Academy, and it was not covered as a DOE, OCR school. I asked if DOE, OCR was the primary office of responsibility for all Title IX compliance reviews. He indicated no, that the executive agency that Youth ChalleNGe was funded under had the responsibility for those compliance reviews (in this case Department of Defense). He asked if the call answered my questions, and I asked that he provide a formal response to my inquiry. He indicated he would, but I have yet to receive any written response.

After learning of the discrepancies relating to schools' implementation of Title IX and the potential impact on schools located on federal installations, I wrote a letter to the United States attorney general requesting she consider modifying 28 CFR 81.2,[6] and to the Commonwealth of Kentucky Attorney General urging his support to modify KRS 620.030 (1), that both include a report to a designated school investigator under Title IX or as a representative under the Equal Employment Opportunity Commission as a legal option for reporting. This effort was undertaken based upon the Assistant District Attorney producing an agreement between Fort Knox and the Kentucky Department of Community Based Services (DCBS) as that designated agency under 42 USC § 13031 to meet these requirements. Initially, 28 CFR 81.2 was invoked to show there was

---

[6]   https://www.law.cornell.edu/cfr/text/28/81.2

no such requirement to involve a designated agency. As indicated in the grand jury questioning, our state appointed Equal Employment Opportunity Commission representative is not a 'criminal' investigator. That the DCBS person receiving any request for review, and making the sole determination that law enforcement should then be contacted, is also not a trained 'criminal' investigator is unbelievable. What makes one non-criminally trained state appointed investigator more capable to determine criminality over the other?

Similarly, I have since written to the Department of Justice, Office of the Inspector General regarding whether it was appropriate for the Office of the District Attorney, Western District of Kentucky not only to ignore the force of law opinion expressed by Assistant Attorney General Virginia Seitz, but to argue against inclusion of the elements of 42 USC § 13031 identified in this opinion. I included the Department of Justice, Office of Legal Counsel, the National Guard Bureau and the Kentucky Department of Military Affairs in this letter as well. I have little hope of receiving a favorable response, based upon the timing of my earlier request to modify 28 CFR 81.2.

Readers will come to realize all the opportunities the prosecution had to correctly withdraw from this effort. There is ample evidence that BCA staff followed the law we knew to follow (Kentucky sexual harassment procedures and Title IX). It seems the assistant district attorneys knew we were also charged under statute that required the attorney general or his representative to train us, to provide a reporting format to us, and to identify to us a designated agency. When it is made known that none of this was ever shared with us, may these actions be identified publically as being inconsistent with the pursuit of justice.

Can any executive agency or the courts proceed to convict any citizen when contravening and legally binding obligation is made known to them? If this can occur in a single case, it can occur in any case. This reality should raise concerns in each of us regarding our federal justice system.

15

EFFORTS TO ACHIEVE FEDERAL TRANSPARENCY

Nothing can destroy a government more quickly
that its failure to observe its own laws, or worse,
its disregard of the character of its existence.

—US Supreme Court Justice Tom C. Clark

You must first enable the government to control
the governed; and in the next place, oblige it to
control itself.

—James Madison

As I have shared throughout this recounting, all the misdemeanor
codefendants followed published policy and procedures regarding the
investigation of sexual harassment complaints. As you can see from
Jane Doe's own post investigator interview statement, she alleges a
sexual harassment incident. At this writing, I have little hope that

any government agency will respond in an appropriate manner to remedy this situation. I will delineate my many efforts here.

I have described the circumstances where the Academy staff initiated and the EEOC representative conducted the sexual harassment investigation previously referenced. This effort, from start to finish, followed the expressed guidance of the program, the Department of Military Affairs, and the Commonwealth of Kentucky. The actions taken in the investigation were exactly as defined in published national Title IX policy. The effort was more immediate and completed much earlier than the defined expectations of Title IX. The outcomes reached mirror exactly what Title IX expects. Both complainants continued in the program. They both graduated. They both graduated at the highest cadet rank. They both participated in sports and service to community activities managed by the respondent in this case. Jane Doe #1 named the respondent as that "staff or cadre having the most positive impact" during her stay at the academy. No additional concerns were expressed by either relating to any other incident of sexual harassment or retaliation on the part of the respondent or anyone who worked for him.

This particular class of female cadets accomplished what no other platoon, male or female, had accomplished before or have accomplished since to my knowledge. Every member of the platoon graduated as a level III cadet, with several earning honor cadet status prior to graduation. I made a photo of this platoon to hang in my office, and to be displayed on the platoon floor.

As another indication of the impact of this investigation on Jane Doe #1, she became eighteen years of age on the weekend following the close of the investigation. Her family came to the Academy for a family birthday party on that weekend. She saw me most work days in the morning medication line, and we discussed many things. I asked on several occasions how she was doing and how Ms. Graves's recommendations were working. She always responded with a smile and insisted that things were fine. I thanked her and every cadet for their smiles—as this is an immediate indication that things are proceeding well for them. She was asked on several occasions if she needed to speak to the counselor; which she declined to do. She was eighteen by this time and had that right. Under HIPPA, we could not even inform her parents that we felt she should see a counselor after her eighteenth birthday. Jane Doe #1 never demonstrated any negative or adverse symptoms from this investigation. After the conclusion of the final meeting in my office, Ms Graves came to me and told me that MSG Onusko had informed her that Jane Doe #1, upon leaving my office and walking to the stairwell at the end of the hall with the cadre, had asked the respondent to adjust the squad leader armband again. The respondent pointed her to the female cadre present to adjust the armband. Ms. Graves indicated this was the final action in this case that confirmed that her assessment and recommendations were correct. These comments were shared in the grand jury comments by both those codefendants.

While we are closing out this part of the Jane Doe #1 experience, let me go on to say that Jane Doe #1, after the investigation, chose not to see the counselor and chose not to tell her parents of the allegation or the investigation. Not only did she not do this at the time but she did not tell them immediately after graduation. She apparently told her parents approximately eighteen months later, probably after receiving a letter from the FBI asking to speak to her about their investigation into that incident. Sometime after receiving this letter, she sought counseling. This counseling went on for a period of time and concluded with a hospital stay where she had an MRI and X-rays. Does this sound like something that was the result of any mental anguish she suffered at the Academy? Was this needed counseling the result of the FBI contacts, at least four instances of different statements being taken? In a letter submitted by the mother to obtain restitution the mother stated, "She (Jane Doe #1) was pursued by the FBI as part of the investigations and as a witness at trial. She didn't ask for any of this. It has been almost three years of pure mental and physical torture for her." Considering that counseling only occurred after probable contact by the FBI and considering this part of the mother's statement, maybe the FBI should be paying the restitution.

I have gone into some detail regarding our investigation following Title IX expectations. Everything I have indicated is true regarding this. At the time, we had no idea what Title IX required, only what our state and department policy required. I learned about Title IX when I began researching the impacts of sexual harassment and schools. There is a large body of case studies available regarding schools and Title IX. When you review this, as I did, you will find that most of Title IX efforts are to insure that schools and school administrators take appropriate action to eliminate or mitigate sexual harassment incidents. While the respondent in Title IX cases may be charged with criminal culpability or can even be sued for civil damages, schools and school administrators who act in accordance with investigation guidelines have general immunity from prosecution or civil damages. Schools that act in an egregious manner, ignoring complainants and not implementing processes and procedures to correct identified behaviors, can be liable. Upon learning of the significance of Title IX, I began searching our contract between the National Guard Bureau and the Commonwealth of Kentucky to determine if and how Title IX applied. In Section 803 of the Master Youth Program Cooperative Agreement, both Title IX and the Civil Rights Act are identified as applying to Youth ChalleNGe. I found it strange that no mention of the sexual harassment implications of Title IX had ever warranted discussion or training at any of the many director workshops I had attended. The only mention of a Title IX–like provision of the contract had been our DMA legal advisor indicating that Title IX prevented Kentucky Youth ChalleNGe from opening a new program in Harlan, Kentucky, for male applicants only. My goal had been to consolidate all female applicants to the program at one location to maximize the economies of scale efficiencies involved. Our normal platoon load of female applicants was about 50 percent of a male platoon. By consolidating all female applicants in one location, I would improve the efficiency of the overall effort. Based on the legal opinion, we not only continued the inefficient 50 percent situation at Fort Knox; we replicated it in Harlan.

Having said all this, Title IX is a much more critical aspect of Youth ChalleNGe than anyone has been trained to consider. The entire premise of Title IX enforcement can be seen at a national level in the recent executive order requiring schools to provide restroom accommodations in all schools based on sexual identification or face withdrawal of federal funding. In the case of Youth ChalleNGe academies, this amounts to 75 percent of their overall funding. Title IX requires a school to conduct a sexual harassment investigation, once an incident is identified. If school authorities think a criminal act has occurred, they can and must involve law enforcement. This involvement does not absolve the school of their Title IX requirement to complete their investigation. Remember, Title IX aims to identify causes and prevent future incidents. From our recent involvement with the courts, I have recommended that all programs respond to all allegations under Title IX guidelines; and once they feel or determine that a crime has been committed, they involve law enforcement immediately (just as I had done both prior to and after the investigation in question). I would go one step further, by obtaining agreement between the designated agency and the academy that the designated agency will review all non-criminal investigations after their completion for sufficiency. In this manner, all allegations are reported to the designated agency. This does not limit the safety of any individual or significantly delay the process regarding any potential victim in the future.

After the grand jury testimony in March, everyone continued their normal day-to-day activities until the world collapsed in late September 2014. The primary defendant's indictment was not a surprise. Six other dedicated people being indicted for failure to report child abuse under 18 USC § 2258 was a shock. I had never heard of this charge. Upon researching the charge, I found that it only applied to covered professionals who worked as an employee or a contractor or operated in a leased facility on a federal government installation (Fort Knox). I later found that this charge is the citation of another law, 42 USC § 13031. This law is the basis for a charge under 18 USC § 2258. Upon reading the primary law, one finds that the legislature included provisions of the law that were expected to be met by the attorney general or their representative. Among these was the identification of a designated agency (supposedly to all covered professionals), the identification of a reporting format, and to the conduct of periodic training. We were later informed that 28 CFR 81.2

met the requirement for the designated agency. 28 CFR 81.2 is not a law. It is an administrative action implemented by Attorney General Janet Reno. Please keep this in mind when considering what both Judge McKinley and Magistrate Judge Lindsay stated regarding their being required to consider executive actions. It seems both chose to include the one while excluding the other.

At no time during my 10.5 year career as director did anyone ever inform me of the existence of 42 USC § 13031, 18 USC § 2258 or 28 CFR 81.2. This included Fort Knox, the provost marshal of Fort Knox, the CID on Fort Knox, the military police on Fort Knox, National Guard Bureau, or the Department of Military Affairs. We were never informed of the existence of a designated agency. We never received a reporting format. We never had any initial or other periodic training. When a rational person reads these requirements, one would expect them to be shared with all covered professionals within a certain specific and exclusive federal installation boundary. One would also think that there are specific agencies that would warrant special attention in this matter. Hospitals, clinics, schools, and Youth ChalleNGe academies would seem to be those places where the required contacts, instruments, and training must occur. I cannot speak to the other locations, but Bluegrass ChalleNGe Academy was never contacted with this information.

Early in the process, maybe December 2014, representatives for some of the other codefendants filed a motion with Judge McKinley to include all elements of 42 USC § 13031 in the indictment in order to provide that an element of mens rea could be established or shown as absent. Judge McKinley ruled against this motion, stating that he felt an element of mens rea was present. The prosecution provided an argument against including the elements of 42 USC § 13031 in the case. Later, my attorney filed a similar motion, as we were not part of the original motion. This motion went before Magistrate Judge Lindsay, and he ruled that he concurred with Judge McKinley's initial ruling. Again, the prosecution argued against the inclusion of any 42 USC § 13031 elements.

As a way of explanation for those of you who don't understand the importance of elements in a trial or of the jury instructions during trial, please consider the following. Once the elements of the crime are established, each of them must be proven to have been violated in order to obtain a guilty verdict. An unproven element in a crime results in a verdict of "not guilty." Had either Judge McKinley or Magistrate Judge Lindsay ruled that the 42 USC § 13031 elements applied, then the prosecution must show that each of us knew of the designated agency, that a reporting format had been provided, and that periodic training had been conducted. If any one of these elements could not be proven to the satisfaction of the judge or jury, then a verdict of "not guilty" must be returned. Since none of them were accomplished, you can understand why the prosecution argued vigorously against their inclusion.

Here is where my research provides another legal concept for your consideration and investigation. As I became aware of the processes relating to elements in cases, motions by both parties, and rulings by the courts, my ability to research became more focused. I am thankful for Internet search engines and the digitization of materials. Fifteen years ago, only a very dedicated legal clerk or paralegal could locate and attempt to understand the mystery of the federal legal process. Today, anyone can research legal arguments.

My research into 42 USC § 13031 resulted in a reference to a Department of Justice, Office of Legal Counsel (DOJ OLC) opinion relating to Veterans Affairs and 42 USC § 13031. I opened this document to find a published opinion by Assistant Attorney General Virginia Seitz in May 2012. This document dealt primarily with a request by Veterans Affairs inquiring that if someone viewed child pornography on their computer, without knowing the age or name of the child, would this be a violation. AAG Seitz began a process to look into this, sending inquiries out to many of the executive agencies and then writing a very complete opinion on the subject of 42USC § 13031. In the body of this opinion, AAG Seitz shares many methods whereby a covered professional might come to be aware of child abuse. She expanded the expectation of responsibility even beyond the borders of the installation and indicated it was not even limited to those who reside on the installation. The most interesting part of the opinion was AAG Seitz agreement that the designated agency element was met by 28 CFR 81.2; however, AAG Seitz then indicates that the elements of reporting format and periodic training must be met before taking any action against any covered professional. As you can imagine, I thought this ended the case against us (or me by this time). As I reviewed the motions from both Judge McKinley and Magistrate Judge Lindsay, I found that they were aware of AAG Seitz opinion and indicated that traditionally the judicial branch has resisted making judgments to motions based upon opinions expressed by the executive branch. In other words, they are not bound by AAG Seitz's opinion. Here again, they included the administrative law expressed by Attorney General Janet Reno in 28 CFR § 81.2 and excluded any consideration of the published force of law opinion expressed by Assistant Attorney General Virginia Seitz.

While this caused me some concern, I wondered how I could ever get anyone to agree to consider common sense in justice. I found that published DOJ OLC opinions have force of law implications on all elements of the executive branch. This includes all the appointed agencies of federal government; DOJ, DOD, HHS, VA, etc. As I considered this, I realized that all offices of the United States Attorney are under the Department of Justice and are therefore legally bound to follow and comply with the AAG Seitz opinion. If someone is legally bound to consider and insure compliance with the reporting format and periodic training elements indicated by AAG Seitz, then, how could that same agency or representative argue against this inclusion? It would seem that law and legal ethics would require the prosecutor's concurrence that these elements are required to be proven! It would seem the prosecutor would be ethically bound to move for dismissal of charges in such circumstances. While the judicial branch may ignore the implications of the executive branch in general practice, how can executive branch agents act in a similar manner?

After the conclusion of the sentencing phase, I wrote to the Department of Justice, Office of the Inspector General, providing enclosures articulating this premise. I provided a copy of this document to the Department of Justice, Office of Legal Counsel for similar review. I provided the document to the National Guard Bureau office with responsibility for the Youth ChalleNGe program and to the Kentucky Department of Military Affairs. At this juncture, the Department of Justice, Office of the Inspector General had replied. They indicated that after reviewing my claim, they determined that theirs was not the correct office to consider the assertion. They indicated they had forwarded my documents to the Department of Justice, Office of Professional Responsibility who was responsible in this case. I hope to report on the responses of these agencies before this book is published.

Throughout the grand jury process of this incident, the person representing the United States Attorney continually asked about Ms. Graves's training and ability to perform a criminal investigation. I shared that she has no such training; rather, she was very qualified to conduct a sexual harassment investigation. This was not only discounted but made to sound like the program was hiding behind the investigation in order to justify our failure to act. This was not the case in any fashion. My staff reacted to information in the exact and proper fashion required. The outcomes of the investigation were painstakingly and thoroughly considered. The outcomes were based on an investigation conducted exactly as expected. The Office of the United States Attorney, through their initial agent, misrepresented the facts to the grand jury. As I realized this, as stated before, I tried to obtain a compliance review of the subject investigation by the Department of Military Affairs, National Guard Bureau, and even the Philadelphia office of the Department of Education, Office of Civil Rights (the responsible agency for Title IX compliance). When the DOE OCR office did not reply to my initial request, I sent a second, including the office of Congressman Brett Guthrie. I reached out and was invited to Congressman Guthrie's Bowling Green office to share my concerns. Congressman Guthrie listened and indicated he wanted to help where he could. I understood he could not become involved with an ongoing trial, but we concluded that he could possibly inquire as to why DOE, OCR had not responded to a request by one of his constituents. Sometime later, I did hear from a representative of DOE, OCR telephonically. I was unable to get his name, but we did have a discussion regarding my request. He indicated that

DOE, OCR only checked compliance on DOE schools and that his investigation showed that Bluegrass ChalleNGe Academy was not a DOE school. I concurred with this, stating that Youth ChalleNGe is under the Department of Defense, one of the executive agencies specifically listed in Title IX governing documents. He also concurred with this, indicating that DOD would have to do the compliance review. I then asked if DOE, OCR along with DOJ, OCR didn't have overall responsibility for compliance under Title IX? He indicated no and asked that if he had answered my question, was there anything further he could do? I asked that he provide a formal response indicating what he had just told me. He asked, 'You want a formal written response?" I responded, "Please." He responded, "Okay," and we concluded the call. I never received that formal written response. I felt that a compliance review of Ms. Graves's Title IX sexual harassment investigation must be held as compliant with Title IX expectations. While the compliance review might recommend that certain allegations, whether founded or unfounded, may be appropriate to share with law enforcement; there would be nothing in this case requiring this action. A compliance review report indicating "compliant" would seem to me to provide evidence that our investigation was accomplishing is a reasonable manner and that we knew what was required. Hopefully this confirmation would provide the court some insight into the legal jeopardy of our situation. How can a person or organization legally and accurately follow the provisions of one law (that they are aware of) and then be found guilty of violation of another law (that we were completely unaware of—even though the law and an executive agency opinion required someone to inform us)?

At this moment, I hope for some response from the Department of Education, The Department of Justice, the National Guard Bureau, or the Department of Military Affairs (or the Kentucky Attorney General).

I wrote to the Department of Justice, Office of the Inspector General, expressing my belief that my civil rights have been violated in that the prosecution not only withheld legally required elements from the jury but also argued against the required elements identified by AAG Seitz even being included. That these elements are legally binding upon the executive agencies and that since neither the reporting format nor the periodic training were accomplished the prosecution clearly withheld exculpatory items of information. To knowingly withhold this from the jury through unlawful characterization seems both insidious and ignoble in its accomplishment. I included the Department of Justice, Office of Legal Counsel, the National Guard Bureau, and the Department of Military Affairs in this mailing. Since the notification that the Office of the Inspector General had forwarded the request to the Office of Professional Responsibility, I am hopeful that all will recognize the inappropriate nature of this action and work to remedy the verdict in some agreeable fashion.

As a speculative departure from those facts shared above, I want to provide some legal concepts for you to consider. Each state and commonwealth in the United States has failure to report child abuse statutes on the books. In Kentucky's case, this law is Kentucky Revised Statute 620.030, titled, Duty to report dependency, neglect, abuse, or human trafficking -- Husband-wife and professional-client/patient privileges not grounds for refusal to report --Exceptions -- Penalties. Since the Assimilative Crimes Act, 18 U.S.C. § 13, allows the federal government to charge any state crime committed on a federal installation, one wonders why 42 USC § 13031, 18 USC § 2258 or 28 CFR 81.2 are even required in the United States? I understand the law may be required for installations in foreign lands, either under military or state department oversight. Whether or not the United States has any recourse in causing any single incident of child abuse that occurred on or off the sovereign premises to be prosecuted in a foreign country, though a covered professional became aware of such an abuse (as the AAG Seitz opinion states) they must still report or face indictment. This is a topic requiring more review within those departments and the Office of Legal Counsel. Since the government can assimilate state crimes, one would imagine this would be the appropriate effort. In Kentucky, this crime is not limited to covered professionals, it applies to anyone. Do we really need multiple means of charging citizens with identical crimes?

As I said, I had no legal training prior to this case, but I became very interested in case law when I faced my first allegation of a crime. While I have endeavored to provide you links to very pertinent information regarding my case; I have not even scratched the surface on how provisions the Administrative Procedures Act (APA) apply in this case, or how the Supreme Court cases and opinions within *Chevron* or *Skidmore* apply. These opinions define what the prosecution cannot withhold regarding evidence that may prove innocence of the accused. If your appetite is whetted by this, I encourage you to also review these opinions to see how they relate. Of course, everyone in this case seems to have felt "it's only a misdemeanor," and little serious investigation into applicable law seems to have occurred. This misdemeanor is attributed to me, and since the consequences are permanent, it takes on special personal meaning. The prosecution wrote an inflammatory and slanted description of the incident from the very beginning and has been able to make this fairy tale become fact in many people's minds. I am hopeful this book will cause some serious review of what has really transpired in this case and may even cause question regarding the why of any misdemeanor indictments in this situation. As you have easily ascertained, there was no basis for any misdemeanor charges to be brought. While it was reported that this indictment was the first such indictment under these obscure and invisible laws, based on the assistant attorney general's language, one can understand why no similar charges have been brought before.

Finally, as I hope you have considered the issues related above, I want you to consider one final argument regarding this case and the court's rulings regarding elements of the case. Consider the difference between a USC (statute) and a CFR (federal regulation). One is congressional law and the other is an administrative action with the force of law to implement the statute. Magistrate Judge Lindsay indicated the courts were not bound by force of law opinions of the Department of Justice Office of Legal Counsel and used the separation of powers as the argument. As you will have discovered when you reviewed the CFR process, these are also administrative actions taken by Executive Branch agencies to implement the law (statute). It seems strange that Magistrate Judge Lindsay would allow 28

CFR 81.2, an administrative action posted to the Code of Federal Regulations on 29 February 1996 by Attorney General Janet Reno to be a fact in the case, while refusing to allow the administrative action posted by Assistant Attorney General Virginia Seitz in a published legal opinion to be included in the case. How is one force of law administrative action different from another? What jurisprudence allows the inclusion of one administrative law and the specific exclusion of another, especially one that provides that no case exists?

One other issue regarding the case that must be settled involves whether a school or governmental contractor on a government installation is obligated to enforce Title IX and whether having done so they gain immunity from prosecution. In every state case involving Title IX, where the organization conducted a reasonable investigation and the outcomes meet the Title IX expectations, this is the outcome. Title IX supersedes or preempts other state law. As a general rule, no one federal law can preempt another. There must be some consideration regarding Title IX and 42 USC §13031, as the circumstances expressed herein clearly indicate the legal tensions where schools are involved.

Justice in America has moved to a point where people of good conscience and faith, following the requirements of a known law, may be charged and convicted of a crime completely unknown to them. This represents just how far from true justice our current system is skewed. Where is the right or wrong in this type justice? Additionally, that the court would consider and include one force of law administrative rule (28 CFR 81.2) while choosing to exclude another force of law published legal opinion (AAG Virginia Seitz, DOJ OLC published opinion) inspires much doubt in a fair process for any of us. How can a court allow one administrative rule and not another? If the constitutional pillars of our public house are equal and balanced; how can the considered rule of the one become abrogated by the other?

Wounded Eagle

The Politically Correct Seduction of the Law in Kentucky

By COL (Ret) John W. Smith

SECTION IV

Extrajudicial Circumstances

16

INDICTMENT DURING A
POLITICAL CAMPAIGN

> Whatever is my right as a man is also the right of
> another, and it becomes my duty to guarantee as
> well as to possess.
>
> —Thomas Paine

As I indicated earlier, most people knew I was campaigning for a
Kentucky state office during 2014. I informed the FBI what I was
doing when they visited my home. I made no effort to hide this from
the grand jury. I conducted my campaign with absolutely no expectation that I would be indicted in any criminal activity.

After the indictment, both our local papers and television
media reported the indictment with multiple articles and inflated
expressions of the charge. The multiple allegations against a primary
individual relating to a 9 August 2013 were conveniently mixed with
another incident that had been properly investigated six months earlier. The earlier staff initiated sexual harassment investigation was
fully investigated and discounted by a lady who had been conducting

these investigations in excess of ten years and who was requested by senior state organizations to participate in other sexual harassment investigations throughout the Commonwealth of Kentucky.

Any candidate for public office places himself in full view of the voting public for thorough review and consideration. In many minds, only the party affiliation matters regarding the sufficiency of a person to represent their views. Our state and national elections are not generally won on the weight of voters who only vote their party affiliation. Elections are won based upon the votes of those who consider the record of an individual and vote accordingly. I did my very best to share the record of a life spent in service; to church, local organizations, state duties, and in defense of my country. I remain proud of my record of achievement. One thing a candidate for any office cannot overcome is that potential October Surprise, whether the allegation is by the other candidate or in this case by the federal prosecutor. Voters who do not personally know the candidate will have doubts based upon these allegations. The simple accusation and constant spreading of the allegation in the media becomes the death knell for the candidate.

During the final month of my campaign, there were many things that were disappointing to me, my family, and my supporters. I was advised by my attorney not to share any specifics of my charge or the circumstances around it. This prevented me from a vigorous campaign to educate the voters on the facts surrounding the allegations. I did share the situation with many who knew me and wanted to try to understand what was happening.

Major General Edward Tonini did not contact me at any time to inquire regarding the charge against me. I was retired at the time of the indictment, and I was unaware before my retirement that any charge would be forthcoming. I could not have known to share anything regarding the charges against me or the other staff beforehand. General Tonini and his public affairs group chose to take the politically correct option for the department and the state. They chose to distance themselves from the allegation by implying that new processes, procedures, and personnel had been put in place to insure nothing like this happens in the future, regardless of the fact that nothing like this had happened in the past 10.5 years either.

The Department of Military Affairs chose to further insulate themselves against the remaining three working employees (Burgess, Graves, and Windom) by placing them on administrative leave with pay when the indictments were announced. Everyone involved in the charge by the grand jury involving Jane Doe #1 had done everything possible to investigate, record, and respond to the young lady who initially only expressed the allegation of sexual harassment to her peers. The staff had done their jobs entirely in accordance with state policy and directives and with Title IX of the Civil Rights Act. They each should have been represented by the Department of Military Affairs attorneys, by the Commonwealth of Kentucky Attorney General, or by National Guard Bureau attorneys. Burgess, Graves, and Windom would be released by the Department of Military Affairs in early 2014, for a misdemeanor indictment based upon an "investigation completed by the United States Attorney." I consider this action disgraceful treatment of loyal employees, who, at that time, were not convicted of any wrong doing. Where is the presumption of innocence until proven guilty in a court of law within the Departments of our Commonwealth? That any employee of the Commonwealth of Kentucky be separated from employment on the basis of a single unproven misdemeanor allegation should be worrisome to all state employees. These same personnel availed themselves of an Alford Plea, which resulted in all charges against them being dismissed, with prejudice in 2016 further shows how ridiculous their termination was. Personnel engaged in public service, performing the known duties of the organization, should expect the loyalty and support of that organization. They were not accused of any overt act; rather they were accused of a crime they didn't even know existed. They were accused of circumstances where they were required to be trained regarding and never were. I hope you feel as much outrage regarding their treatment as I do! These three state personnel were dedicated to the program and performing in an exemplary manner. I know this to be true as I witnessed their performance on a daily basis.

Immediately following the indictment and after much previous support from my state Democratic party, they requested I withdraw from the election. No one from the party leadership ever asked about the nature of the charges against me. I shared that I was innocent of all charges and that I had the right to expect the presumption of innocence by everyone involved and would not withdraw from the campaign based simply on an allegation. I was informed by the Democrat party chairman that if I chose to continue this course, that the Kentucky Democrat Party would publically call for my withdrawal, would withdraw support from my campaign, and would provide no future financial support. I declined to withdraw, and the party chairman was true to his word and this press release was new fodder for the media. Additionally, within two days of this statewide press release all support from the Warren County Democrat Party ceased, and all materials I had provided to the county party headquarters for distribution through volunteers disappeared.

During this period, I was advised of comments made by people I had known most of my life regarding my circumstance. Some of these comments were so disappointing that I choose not to share them, other than to note there remains a permanent scar. My family and I have been deeply hurt but have moved on and continue cordial relations with these few, but I think we are all aware of the permanent scar.

Of positive note, those who really know me, my family, and my entire life's work stood behind us all the way through and beyond the election. I was disappointed that we did not win; however, the outcome was preordained at the moment an indictment was announced. The fact that I received almost five thousand votes in an election against an incumbent, after an indictment in federal court, and after the Kentucky Democrat party and Warren Democrat County party withdrew any support for me as a testament to those who knew me and continued their unwavering support. I want to publically thank the Edmonson County Democrat Party leadership for their unwavering and continuing support. Deserving of special recognition is Mr. Dennis Hunley. He is the holder of a debt I can never repay. I would also like to thank Kentucky House Speaker Greg Stumbo for his message of encouragement and support in my darkest time. I would also like to thank Mr. Roger Thomas for his unwavering support during the entire campaign. I worried that my decisions would place him at grave political risk, but he consistently admonished me to do what I felt was right and not worry about him.

Since the time of this initial indictment, a campaign cycle has passed; and during 2016, no one filed to run against the current state representative of District 19. I inquired to both the Warren and Edmonson County Executive Committees and found that no opposition was willing to enter the contest. After consulting with Speaker Stumbo, former Speaker Richards, and others regarding the party not repeating what had happened in the last election cycle, I filed as a Democrat candidate again. I feel that every citizen should have the opportunity to vote for more than one person in each election cycle. I entered this race with a much different attitude than the last. I am wiser and more readily accept the role of God in my life. I trusted and prayed that God would give me the strength and support to succeed in the last election, but in truth I felt that if I worked hard enough and gained enough support, I would be elected. I fully trust in God during this election. I hope to be able to represent and work for the people of Warren and Edmonson County to accomplish good for them. If they don't realize this already, and if God doesn't lead them to this decision in their heart, then my candidacy is not in the direction God has in mind for me. I am completely at peace and trusting in this.

17

THE FUTURE

Always seek justice, but love mercy. To love justice and hate mercy is but a doorway to more injustice.

—Criss Jami

This book has been intended as a vehicle to share the message of what has happened in my life since September 2014 and my efforts before and since that date. I hope all the readers' research, conducted after reading this book to verify everything I have indicated in these pages is beneficial and insightful.

The only personal gain I plan to receive from the publication of this book is the knowledge that my future descendants will have a resource to understand what happened that led their grandfather, however many times removed, to have a single blemish on his public record. I have tried to live a life worthy of emulation by my current and future descendants. I know that all the press releases regarding this trial will be embedded within our internet, our cloud or whatever descriptor that will follow for all time. Publishing this work is the only means to counteract the very one-sided attack message shared and then printed against me. Our justice system is an "adversarial" system by definition. I use the word *attack* as a very apt descriptor of the pretrial adversarial process used by prosecutors.

I would like to thank many people as I close this book. I would like to thank my wife, LaDonna, for her steadfast support and presence beside me. She had participated in much of the research, and her many questions and logical expression of our personal freedoms became a point of departure for my research into an issue. I would like to thank my children for their support and their explanations to their children about this process. I want to thank family and friends for reviewing the initial draft of the book, and for their recommendations to improve the text. I want to thank my family, former military comrades, former Youth ChalleNGe staff acquaintances (both from Kentucky and nationally), and my local church fellowship for all the expressions of support during this time. I would like to thank Darren Wolff for his advice, consideration, counsel and representation. Mr. Wolff, upon receiving all the letters during presentencing, expressed that he had never witnessed this type of support. I shared that it was both very humbling and very moving. He indicated I should be very happy, and he likened me to George Bailey in *It's a Wonderful Life*. George was a person who dedicated his life to helping others and in a low point in life, when circumstances seemed to indicate he had done something wrong, he was able to witness the love and caring of those around him. I thank him very much for that expression of kindness. "Mr. Wolff never knew the personal connection this reference had for me. During my second class, Lieutenant Colonel Jim Cook donated a small brass bell to BCA. That class of cadets named the bell Independence, and our trades class constructed a base for the bell. At the end of every graduation, each graduate crossed the stage after I presented them their diploma. The graduates shook hands with the official party, crossed the stage, and rang the bell one time as a symbol of their accomplishment and the finality of their Youth ChalleNGe experience. I always hoped that every bell they heard in the future would remind them of that moment of accomplishment. That upon hearing a bell ringing, they would be reminded of their accomplishment and know that other subsequent cadets had earned their wings.

I want to once again thank those soldiers and professionals who responded to my request to act as character witnesses during my trial: Major General Michael W. Davidson, Major General Donald Storm, Chaplain (Brigadier General) Patrick Dolan, Dr. Mary Benson, Colonel Joe Warren, Lieutenant Colonel Jim Cook, Command Sergeant Major Edgar Satchwell, and Command Sergeant Major Thomas Pendleton (though illness prevented him from appearing at the trial). I also wish to thank Major General Davidson for challenging me as a young field grade officer to excel and for requiring me and other young Kentucky National Guard leaders to train for and complete the US Army Air Assault Course as an example of leadership (I remain very fond of my cohort graduating class.), for selecting me ahead of the zone for Battalion Command, for volunteering our Battalion to represent Kentucky and our nation as only one of four combat arms National Guard Battalions to serve in Operation Desert Storm, and for his quiet assistance with legal 'free' advice after the trial.

I continue to request review by the United States Department of Justice regarding the apparent disregard of the force of law requirements by the prosecutors in this case. The Department of Justice indicated they could not respond because further litigation seemed to be indicated. It has become apparent to me that this department should be renamed the Department of Litigation, as the obvious injustice of the situation may never be confirmed. I am reminded of the national security response, "I can neither confirm nor deny". Must injustice prevail in the absence of litigation?

Finally, I want to thank each of you for taking time to read this book to this point. I worry that many will not read this far, but I am glad you did. I urge you to check every bit of research I share in this book. I also urge you to get involved with your legislator to request the changes recommended in this book to update the grand jury process, and to hopefully recognize the trained and designated Title IX investigators in schools around our nation as qualified to perform their jobs.

I do, and will continue to, recite our Pledge of Allegiance to the Flag as it is written. My hope is that "with justice for all" becomes the reality someday soon. No outcome in any court will ever diminish my knowledge and belief that I have always executed my duties in an honorable manner, striving as the West Point Cadet's prayer states, "To always choose the harder right over the easier wrong.' I believe that the majority of my staff, whether in the military or Youth ChalleNGe; recognized and adopted this same trait.

TABLE OF
APPENDIXES

A1

THE INITIAL PRESS RELEASE REGARDING THE INDICTMENT

FOR IMMEDIATE RELEASE

Monday, September 29, 2014

Former Police Officer And School Administrator Charged With Violating Federal Child Sex Abuse Laws Other School Officials Charged With Failing To Report The Abuse

LOUISVILLE, Ky. – A federal grand jury charged a Grayson County, Kentucky, man with violating federal laws designed to protect children from sexual abuse as well as threatening/intimidating a witness. The grand jury also charged several other school officials with failing to report the abuse, announced David J. Hale, United States Attorney for the Western District of Kentucky.

Stephen E. Miller, age 44, previously worked as a police officer in Leitchfield, Kentucky. He resigned the position following complaints of inappropriate sexual activity toward two women. Miller then began working at Bluegrass Challenge Academy, a residential, educational program run by the Kentucky National Guard, located on Fort Knox Military Base. Miller had supervisory authority over the Academy students. He is charged with engaging in sexual contact with three students, including an incident of aggravated sexual abuse with one of the three. The incidents occurred between February and August, 2013. The Indictment also charges Miller with attempting to threaten or intimidate the third student to prevent her from reporting the matter to law enforcement.

Additionally, the grand jury charged school officials, John W. Smith, Leroy Burgess, Jr., Kemmye S. Graves, Rolanshia Windom, Rita Carthen, and Gabriel Onusko with failing to report the first incident of abuse to law enforcement officials, as required by federal law.

If convicted, Miller faces a maximum sentence of life in prison, a fine of up to $1,250,000 and at least five years of supervised release. The remaining defendants, if convicted, face maximum sentences of one year in prison, a fine of up to $100,000 and up to one year of supervised release. Miller is being held in the custody of the United States Marshals Service.

Assistant United States Attorneys Jo E. Lawless and Stephanie Zimdahl are prosecuting the case. The Federal Bureau of Investigation (FBI) with assistance from the Army Criminal Investigation Division conducted the investigation.

The indictment of a person by a Grand Jury is an accusation only and that person is presumed innocent until and unless proven guilty.

A2

JOHN WAYNE SMITH
CAMPAIGN PRESS RELEASE

JOHN WAYNE SMITH FOR STATE REPRESENTATIVE

To the Citizens of Kentucky House District 19: After much prayer, discussions with family and the urgings of friends and supporters, I have decided to remain in the campaign to represent the people of Kentucky's 19th House District. I am innocent of the charge filed against me which consists of one single misdemeanor count stemming from the alleged wrongdoing of another individual under my command while I served as Director, Bluegrass ChalleNGe Academy. An innocent person who waivers at the first instance of false accusation or criticism would be unworthy to be called your representative.

I have always been committed to doing the right thing for those I worked with and represented; whether that was in school, at Holley, the Battalion, the Kentucky Military Academy, as Chief of Staff of the Kentucky National Guard or as Director of the Bluegrass ChalleNGe Academy. Every person who came into contact with me in these duties knows this to be true. Every staff member, cadet, and family member of former cadets knows I worked to create the very best of opportunities in their lives.

We are a nation of traditions, truth, caring, standards and compassion. We have a system of justice that is blind and presumes a person's innocence until a group of his or her peers determines otherwise. I only ask that you remember this in the coming weeks and months. You need no warning to understand that the political machines operating in our country today ignore any presumption of innocence and work to cast doubt and distrust at every opportunity. I know the people I am working to represent recognize these attacks for what they are and hope any future attacks regarding these allegations cause those listening, reading or watching to be resolved to vote against smear tactics. I stand on my record of performance, accomplishment, service and character.

While I am disappointed in the Kentucky Democratic Party in calling on me to withdraw from this campaign, I fully appreciate their concerns relating to experienced negative campaigning. I pray that every voter in District 19, and in Kentucky, recognizes this effort for what it is and that each reference that challenges my innocence in this matter results in more people expressing their dissatisfaction with these tactics through their votes. I advised the Kentucky Democratic Party that while I appreciate their concerns, my first priority is to represent the wishes of the citizens of District 19— before and after this election. I will not resign from this race with the overwhelming support I am getting from members of all parties within this district.

This morning, as I considered the challenges of the past week, I was reminded of the verses in Daniel, Chapter 3. I knew there would be heat and fire associated with a campaign for state office. I never thought I would be cast into that fiery furnace, one so hot that my guards and even my guardians are burnt away. Like Daniel reported, I know I am not alone in the furnace! I know I am innocent and I trust in God to bring me from this furnace unmarked.

Thank you for the outpourings of support, encouragement and prayer. Please keep me, my family and all those involved in your continued prayers.

John Wayne Smith   Paid for by John Wayne Smith

A3

18 UNITED STATES CODE (USC) § 2258

(https://www.law.cornell.edu/uscode/text/18/2258)

18 U.S. Code § 2258 - Failure to report child abuse

A person who, while engaged in a professional capacity or activity described in subsection (b) of section 226 of the Victims of Child Abuse Act of 1990 on Federal land or in a federally operated (or contracted) facility, learns of facts that give reason to suspect that a child has suffered an incident of child abuse, as defined in subsection (c) of that section, and fails to make a timely report as required by subsection (a) of that section, shall be fined under this title or imprisoned not more than 1 year or both.

(Added Pub. L. 101–647, title II, § 226(g)(1), Nov. 29, 1990, 104 Stat. 4808; amended Pub. L. 109–248, title II, § 209, July 27, 2006, 120 Stat. 615.)

A4

42 UNITED STATES CODE (USC) § 13031

(https://www.law.cornell.edu/uscode/text/42/13031)

42 U.S. Code § 13031 - Child abuse reporting

(a) In general

A person who, while engaged in a professional capacity or activity described in subsection (b) of this section on Federal land or in a federally operated (or contracted) facility, learns of facts that give reason to suspect that a child has suffered an incident of child abuse, shall as soon as possible make a report of the suspected abuse to the agency designated under subsection (d) of this section.

(b) Covered professionals

Persons engaged in the following professions and activities are subject to the requirements of subsection (a) of this section:

(1) Physicians, dentists, medical residents or interns, hospital personnel and administrators, nurses, health care practitioners, chiropractors, osteopaths, pharmacists, optometrists, podiatrists, emergency medical technicians, ambulance drivers, undertakers, coroners, medical examiners, alcohol or drug treatment personnel, and persons performing a healing role or practicing the healing arts.

(2) Psychologists, psychiatrists, and mental health professionals.

(3) Social workers, licensed or unlicensed marriage, family, and individual counselors.

(4) Teachers, teacher's aides or assistants, school counselors and guidance personnel, school officials, and school administrators.

(5) Child care workers and administrators.

(6) Law enforcement personnel, probation officers, criminal prosecutors, and juvenile rehabilitation or detention facility employees.

(7) Foster parents.

(8) Commercial film and photo processors.

(c) Definitions

For the purposes of this section—

(1) the term "child abuse" means the physical or mental injury, sexual abuse or exploitation, or negligent treatment of a child;

(2) the term "physical injury" includes but is not limited to lacerations, fractured bones, burns, internal injuries, severe bruising or serious bodily harm;

(3) the term "mental injury" means harm to a child's psychological or intellectual functioning which may be exhibited by severe anxiety, depression, withdrawal or outward aggressive behavior, or a combination of those behaviors, which may be demonstrated by a change in behavior, emotional response or cognition;

(4) the term "sexual abuse" includes the employment, use, persuasion, inducement, enticement, or coercion of a child to engage in, or assist another person to engage in, sexually explicit conduct or the rape, molestation, prostitution, or other form of sexual exploitation of children, or incest with children;

(5) the term "sexually explicit conduct" means actual or simulated—

    (A) sexual intercourse, including sexual contact in the manner of genital-genital, oral-genital, anal-genital, or oral-anal contact, whether between persons of the same or of opposite sex; sexual contact means the intentional touching, either directly or through clothing, of the genitalia, anus, groin, breast, inner thigh, or buttocks of any person with an intent to abuse, humiliate, harass, degrade, or arouse or gratify sexual desire of any person;

    (B) bestiality;

    (C) masturbation;

    (D) lascivious exhibition of the genitals or pubic area of a person or animal; or

    (E) sadistic or masochistic abuse;

(6) the term "exploitation" means child pornography or child prostitution;

(7) the term "negligent treatment" means the failure to provide, for reasons other than poverty, adequate food, clothing, shelter, or medical care so as to seriously endanger the physical health of the child; and

(8) the term "child abuse" shall not include discipline administered by a parent or legal guardian to his or her child provided it is reasonable in manner and moderate in degree and otherwise does not constitute cruelty.

(d) Agency designated to receive report and action to be taken
For all Federal lands and all federally operated (or contracted) facilities in which children are cared for or reside, the Attorney General shall designate an agency to receive and investigate the reports described in subsection (a) of this section. By formal written agreement, the designated agency may be a non-Federal agency. When such reports are received by social services or health care agencies, and involve allegations of sexual abuse, serious physical injury, or life-threatening neglect of a child, there shall be an immediate referral of the report to a law enforcement agency with authority to take emergency action to protect the child. All reports received shall be promptly investigated, and whenever appropriate, investigations shall be conducted jointly by social services and law enforcement personnel, with a view toward avoiding unnecessary multiple interviews with the child.

(e) Reporting form
In every federally operated (or contracted) facility, and on all Federal lands, a standard written reporting form, with instructions, shall be disseminated to all mandated reporter groups. Use of the form shall be encouraged, but its use shall not take the place of the immediate making of oral reports, telephonically or otherwise, when circumstances dictate.

(f) Immunity for good faith reporting and associated actions
All persons who, acting in good faith, make a report by subsection (a) of this section, or otherwise provide information or assistance in connection with a report, investigation, or legal intervention pursuant to a report, shall be immune from civil and criminal liability arising out of such actions. There shall be a presumption that any such persons acted in good faith. If a person is sued because of the person's performance of one of the above functions,

and the defendant prevails in the litigation, the court may order that the plaintiff pay the defendant's legal expenses. Immunity shall not be accorded to persons acting in bad faith.

(g) Omitted

(h) Training of prospective reporters

All individuals in the occupations listed in subsection (b)(1) of this section who work on Federal lands, or are employed in federally operated (or contracted) facilities, shall receive periodic training in the obligation to report, as well as in the identification of abused and neglected children.

Source

(Pub. L. 101–647, title II, § 226,Nov. 29, 1990, 104 Stat. 4806.)

Codification

Section is comprised of section 226 of Pub. L. 101–647. Subsec. (g) of section 226 of Pub. L. 101–647enacted section 2258 of Title 18, Crimes and Criminal Procedure.

This is a list of parts within the Code of Federal Regulations for which this US Code section provides rulemaking authority.

This list is taken from the Parallel Table of Authorities and Rules provided by GPO [Government Printing Office].

It is not guaranteed to be accurate or up-to-date, though we do refresh the database weekly. More limitations on accuracy are described at the GPO site.

Hide 28 CFR - Judicial Administration

28 CFR Part 81 - CHILD ABUSE AND CHILD PORNOGRAPHY REPORTING DESIGNATIONS AND PROCEDURES

A5

28 CODE OF FEDERAL REGULATIONS (CFR) § 81.2

(https://www.law.cornell.edu/cfr/text/28/81.2)

28 CFR 81.2 - Submission of reports; designation of agencies to receive reports of child abuse.

Reports of child abuse required by 42 U.S.C. 13031 shall be made to the local law enforcement agency or local child protective services agency that has jurisdiction to investigate reports of child abuse or to protect child abuse victims in the land area or facility in question. Such agencies are hereby respectively designated as the agencies to receive and investigate such reports, pursuant to 42 U.S.C. 13031(d), with respect to federal lands and federally operated or contracted facilities within their respective jurisdictions, provided that such agencies, if non-federal, enter into formal written agreements to do so with the Attorney General, her delegate, or a federal agency with jurisdiction for the area or facility in question. If the child abuse reported by the covered professional pursuant to 42 U.S.C. 13031 occurred outside the federal area or facility in question, the designated local law enforcement agency or local child protective services agency receiving the report shall immediately forward the matter to the appropriate authority with jurisdiction outside the federal area in question.

A6

Department Of Justice Office of Legal Counsel Published Opinion Regarding 42 USC § 13031

(https://www.justice.gov/sites/default/files/olc/opinions/2012/05
/31/aag-reporting-abuse.pdf)

Duty to Report Suspected Child Abuse Under
42 U.S.C. § 13031

Under 42 U.S.C. § 13031—a provision of the Victims of Child Abuse Act of 1990—all covered professionals who learn of suspected child abuse while engaged in enumerated activities and professions on federal land or in federal facilities must report that abuse, regardless of where the suspected victim is cared for or resides.

The fact that a patient has viewed child pornography may "give reason to suspect that a child has suffered an incident of child abuse" under the statute, and a covered professional is not relieved of an obligation to report the possible abuse simply because neither the covered professional nor the patient knows the identity of the child depicted in the pornography.

May 29, 2012

MEMORANDUM OPINION FOR
THE GENERAL COUNSEL
UNITED STATES DEPARTMENT OF VETERANS AFFAIRS

Section 13031 of title 42, a provision in the Victims of Child Abuse Act of 1990 ("VCAA" or "Act"), Pub. L. No. 101-647, tit. II, § 226, 104 Stat. 4789, 4806, requires persons engaged in certain activities and professions on federal lands or in federal facilities to report "facts that give reason to suspect that a child has suffered an incident of child abuse" if they learn such facts in the course of their professional activities. Failure to make a report required by section 13031 could subject such persons to criminal penalties. See 18 U.S.C. § 2258 (2006). You have raised two questions about the scope of section 13031. See Letter for the Honorable Eric Holder, Attorney General, from Will A. Gunn, General Counsel, Department of Veterans Affairs (Nov. 9, 2009) ("VA Letter").

First, you have asked whether section 13031's reporting requirement is limited to situations in which the suspected victim of child abuse is cared for or resides on federal land or in a federal facility. We conclude that it is not. Instead, under the VCAA, all persons who learn of suspected child abuse (as defined by the Act) while engaged in the enumerated activities and professions on federal land or in federal facilities must report that abuse, regardless of where the suspected victim is cared for or resides. We recognize that the scope of some of the statutory language may be ambiguous, and that narrower readings of the reporting requirement find some support in certain of the statute's provisions. But we believe that section 13031, read as a whole and in light of its purpose, is best interpreted broadly.

Second, you have inquired whether the VCAA's reporting obligation is triggered when a person covered by section 13031 learns that a patient under his or her care has viewed child pornography, even if the person does not know, and has no reason to believe the patient knows, the identity of the child or children depicted in the pornography. We conclude that the fact that a patient has viewed child pornography may be a "fact[] . . . giv[ing] reason to suspect that a child has suffered an incident of child abuse" under section 13031, and that the statute does not require a covered professional to possess knowledge of the identity of an affected child in order for the reporting duty to apply.

We have concluded that the interpretive questions you have raised can be resolved using ordinary tools of statutory construction, so we have not applied the rule of lenity even though the VCAA provides for criminal penalties. We note, however, that a person who fails to make a report required by section 13031 will not necessarily be subject to criminal penalties under the statute. The criminal penalty provision contains no explicit mens rea requirement, and thus one would almost certainly be inferred. See United States v. X-Citement Video, Inc., 513 U.S. 64, 70 (1994). While we need not decide what mens rea would apply, a court construing section 13031 might well require a defendant to have known that a report was legally required before imposing criminal liability for a failure to report. Such a reading would, among other things, address any concern about imposing criminal liability on persons who lacked clear notice that the failure to report in their particular circumstances was unlawful.

I.

Congress enacted the VCAA, including section 13031, as title II of the Crime Control Act of 1990. Pub. L. No. 101-647, §§ 201-255, 104 Stat. at 4792-4815. Section 13031 requires persons on "Federal land or in a federally operated (or contracted) facility" who are engaged in certain activities—individuals the statute calls "[c]overed professionals"—to report suspected incidents of child abuse. 42 U.S.C. § 13031(a)-(b) (2006). Specifically, section 13031(a) provides that [a] person who, while engaged in a professional capacity or activity described in subsection (b) of this section on Federal land or in a federally operated (or contracted) facility, learns of facts that give reason to suspect that a child has suffered an incident of child abuse, shall as soon as possible make a report of the suspected abuse to the agency designated under subsection (d) of this section. Id. § 13031(a)₁

---

[1]Subsection (b) provides:

Persons engaged in the following professions and activities are subject to the requirements of subsection (a) of this section:

(1) Physicians, dentists, medical residents or interns, hospital personnel and administrators, nurses, health care practitioners, chiropractors, osteopaths, pharmacists, optometrists, podiatrists, emergency medical technicians, ambulance drivers, undertakers, coroners, medical examiners, alcohol or drug treatment personnel, and persons performing a healing role or practicing the healing arts.

(2) Psychologists, psychiatrists, and mental health professionals

(3) Social workers, licensed or unlicensed marriage, family, and individual counselors.

(4) Teachers, teacher's aides or assistants, school counselors and guidance personnel, school officials, and school administrators.

(5) Child care workers and administrators.

(6) Law enforcement personnel, probation officers, criminal prosecutors, and juvenile rehabilitation or detention facility employees.

(7) Foster parents.

(8) Commercial film and photo processors.

42 U.S.C. § 13031(b).

Duty to Report Suspected Child Abuse Under 42 U.S.C. § 13031

Section 13031(d) directs the Attorney General to designate the agency or agencies to which the reports described in subsection (a) should be made. It states:

> For all Federal lands and all federally operated (or contracted) facilities in which children are cared for or reside, the Attorney General shall designate an agency to receive and investigate the reports described in subsection (a) of this section. By formal written agreement, the designated agency may be a non-Federal agency. When such reports are received by social services or health care agencies, and involve allegations of sexual abuse, serious physical injury, or life-threatening neglect of a child, there shall be an immediate referral of the report to a law enforcement agency with authority to take emergency action to protect the child. All reports received shall be promptly investigated, and whenever appropriate, investigations shall be conducted jointly by social services and law enforcement personnel, with a view toward avoiding unnecessary multiple interviews with the child.

Id. § 13031(d) (2006).

Consistent with this directive, the Attorney General has issued a regulation designating the agencies authorized to receive and investigate reports of child abuse submitted under section 13031(a). That rule, which appears as 28 C.F.R. § 81.2 (2010), provides:

> Reports of child abuse required by 42 U.S.C. 13031 shall be made to the local law enforcement agency or local child protective services agency that has jurisdiction to investigate reports of child abuse or to protect child abuse victims in the land area or facility in question.

Such agencies are hereby respectively designated as the agencies to receive and investigate such reports, pursuant to 42 U.S.C. 13031(d), with respect to federal lands and federally operated or contracted facilities within their respective jurisdictions, provided that such agencies, if non-federal, enter into formal written agreements to do so with the Attorney General, her delegate, or a federal agency with jurisdiction for the area or facility in question. If the child abuse reported by the covered professional pursuant to 42 U.S.C. 13031 occurred outside the federal area or facility in question, the designated local law enforcement agency or local child protective services agency receiving the report shall immediately forward the matter to the appropriate authority with jurisdiction outside the federal area in question.

Att'y Gen. Order No. 2009-96, 61 Fed. Reg. 7704 (Feb. 29, 1996).

Under section 13031, "the term 'child abuse' means the physical or mental injury, sexual abuse or exploitation, or negligent treatment of a child." 42 U.S.C. § 13031(c)(1) (2006). Section 13031 further explains that the term 'sexual abuse' includes the employment, use, persuasion, inducement, enticement, or coercion of a child to engage in, or assist another person to engage in, sexually explicit conduct or the rape, molestation, prostitution, or other form of sexual exploitation of children, or incest with children.

Id. § 13031(c)(4) (2006). "[T]he term 'exploitation' means child pornography or child prostitution." Id. § 13031(c)(6) (2006).

Two other provisions in section 13031 are also relevant. Section 13031(e) provides that "[i]n every federally operated (or contracted) facility, and on all federal lands, a standard written reporting form, with instructions, shall be disseminated to all mandated reporter groups," and makes clear as well that although "[u]se of the form shall be encouraged, . . . its use shall not take the place of the immediate making of oral reports . . . when circumstances dictate." Id. § 13031(e). Section 13031(h) provides that "[a]ll individuals in the occupations listed in subsection (b)(1) of this section who work on Federal lands, or are employed in federally operated (or contracted) facilities, shall receive periodic training in the obligation to report, as well as in the identification of abused and neglected children." Id. § 13031(h).

Finally, in section 226(g)(1) of the VCAA, codified as amended at 18 U.S.C. § 2258, Congress criminalized the failure to report child abuse as mandated by 42 U.S.C. § 13031. The criminal provision states:

A person who, while engaged in a professional capacity or activity described in subsection (b) of section 226 of the Victims of Child Abuse Act of 1990 [42 U.S.C. § 13031] on Federal land or in a federally operated (or contracted) facility, learns of facts that give reason to suspect that a child has suffered an incident of child abuse, as defined in subsection (c) of that section, and fails to make a timely report as required by subsection (a) of that section, shall be fined under this title or imprisoned not more than 1 year or both.

18 U.S.C. § 2258. When the VCAA was originally enacted, the offense was a Class B misdemeanor punishable by six months of imprisonment, id. § 226(g)(1), 104 Stat. at 4808; 18 U.S.C. § 3581(b)(7) (1988), but in 2006, Congress amended 18 U.S.C. § 2258 by raising the maximum punishment from six months to one year of imprisonment. Adam Walsh Child Protection and Safety Act of 2006, Pub. L. No. 109-248, § 209, 120 Stat. 587, 615. Other than this change, Congress has amended neither 18 U.S.C. § 2258 nor 42 U.S.C. § 13031 since it enacted the provisions in 1990.

II.

A.

We first consider the circumstances under which covered professionals must report suspected child abuse under the VCAA.2We conclude that, although no interpretation of section 13031 perfectly reconciles all of its provisions, section 13031 is best read to impose a reporting obligation on all persons who, while engaged in the covered professions and activities on federal lands or in federal facilities, learn of facts that give reason to suspect that child abuse has occurred, regardless of where the abuse might have occurred or where the suspected victim is cared for or resides. In reaching this conclusion, we considered the construction of section 13031 that you propose, as well as two other readings that would narrow the reporting obligation. As explained below, while all of these narrowing constructions find support in certain provisions of the statute, they are also in significant tension with other parts of section 13031, leading us to conclude that section 13031 "'as a whole'" is best read to impose the broad reporting obligation described above. See United States v. Atlantic Research Corp., 551 U.S. 128, 135 (2007) (quoting King v. St. Vincent's Hospital, 502 U.S. 215, 221 (1991)).

---

[2]In preparing our opinion, we considered views provided by your office, the Department of Justice's Criminal Division, the Department of Defense, the Department of State, and the Attorney General's Advisory Council. See E-mail for Jeannie S. Rhee, Deputy Assistant Attorney General, Office of Legal Counsel ("OLC"), from Alexandra Gelber, Criminal Division (Jan. 15, 2010 10:15 AM); E-mail for Jeannie S. Rhee, Deputy Assistant Attorney General, OLC, from John Casciotti, Office of General Counsel, Dep't of Defense (Feb. 26, 2010 5:02 PM); E-mail for Jeannie S. Rhee, Deputy Assistant Attorney General, OLC, from Robert Choo, Office of the Legal Adviser, Dep't of State (July 21, 2010 2:35 PM); E-mail for Cristina M. Rodríguez, Deputy Assistant Attorney General, Benjamin Mizer,

Senior Counsel, and Matthew Roberts, Senior Counsel, OLC, from Carter Stewart, United States Attorney for the Southern District of Ohio (Feb. 3, 2012 6:45 PM). We also solicited the opinion of the Department of Health and Human Services, which indicated that it "has no view about the interpretation advanced by the Veterans Administration." E-mail for Jeannie S. Rhee, Deputy Assistant Attorney General, OLC, from Elizabeth J. Gianturco, Senior Advisor to the General Counsel, Dep't of Health and Human Servs. (Apr. 21, 2010 2:16 PM).

Section 13031(a) sets forth the reporting requirement that is the VCAA's core directive. It provides that a covered professional engaged in a covered activity "on Federal land or in a federally operated (or contracted) facility" who "learns of facts that give reason to suspect that a child has suffered an incident of child abuse, shall as soon as possible make a re

port of the suspected abuse to the agency designated under subsection (d) of this section." 42 U.S.C. § 13031(a). On its face, this is a broad provision: It applies to covered professionals on all federal lands and in all federal facilities and requires a report as soon as possible no matter where the suspected child victim resides, is cared for, or may have been abused.

The express incorporation of subsection (d), however, gives rise to doubt about the scope of subsection (a)'s reporting requirement, because subsection (d) appears to require the Attorney General to designate an agency to receive reports only "[f]or all Federal lands and all federally operated (or contracted) facilities in which children are cared for or reside." Id. § 13031(d) (emphasis added). The central question, then, is whether the cross-reference to subsection (d) limits subsection (a)'s otherwise broad language, and if so, in what way.[3]

You suggest that it would be reasonable to read the reporting requirement as applying "only with regard to suspected abuse of children residing or cared for on Federal lands and in federally operated and contracted facilities," because "42 U.S.C. § 13031(a) requires reporting only to agencies as designated under subsection (d), and subsection (d) provides for designation only of agencies to receive and investigate reports for Federal reservations in which children are cared for or reside." VA Letter at 2. In other words, you maintain that, because subsection (d) specifies agencies to receive reports only for "Federal lands and . . . facilities in which children are cared for or reside," 42 U.S.C. § 13031(d), Congress intended to require

---

3We assume for purposes of this opinion, as do you, that the phrase "in which children are cared for or reside" modifies both "Federal lands" and "federally operated (or contracted) facilities." VA Letter at 2 ("subsection (d) provides for designation . . . of agencies to receive and investigate reports for Federal reservations in which children are cared for or reside"). The Attorney General's regulations do not address the issue, 28 C.F.R. pt. 81 (2010), nor do any of the submissions we received. Reports only for suspected abuse of children who reside or are cared for on federal lands or in federal facilities. Moreover, it might be argued that when the Attorney General designates an agency to receive reports for Federal lands and facilities in which children are not cared for and do not reside, he is not making designations "under" subsection (d), because that provision expressly addresses designations only for federal lands and facilities "in which children are cared for or reside." Id. This construction of section 13031, in your view, would appropriately align the location of the suspected child victims with subsection (d)'s designation of agencies to receive reports.

This interpretation is not without some force, but we believe it is inconsistent with other subsections of section 13031 and with the statute viewed in its entirety. See Davis v. Mich. Dep't of Treasury, 489 U.S. 803, 809 (1989) ("It is a fundamental canon of statutory construction that the words of a statute must be read in their context and with a view to their place in the overall statutory scheme."). As noted above, Congress phrased subsection (a) using broad language that contains no limitation on the federal lands or facilities in which reporting is required, and no residence-based limitation on the suspected child victims whose potential abuse can give rise to a reporting obligation. 42 U.S.C. § 13031(a). In fact, section 13031 as a whole is devoid of any language that explicitly limits the suspected child victims whose potential abuse triggers the reporting requirement.

If Congress had intended to limit the scope of the VCAA's reporting requirement in the significant manner you propose, an isolated cross-reference to subsection (d) would have been an obscure and backhanded way to do so. Cf. Allied Chem. & Alkali Workers Local 1 v. Pittsburgh Plate Glass Co., 404 U.S. 157, 170-71 (1971) ("To accept the Board's reasoning that the union's § 302(c)(5) responsibilities dictate the scope of the § 8(a)(5) collective bargaining obligation would be to allow the tail to wag the dog."). Subsection (d) is entitled "[a]gency designated to receive report and action to be taken," and purports to address only the agencies to which reports must be made, not the professionals who must make reports or the children who may be the subject of reports. Nothing in subsection (d) expressly narrows the scope of potential child victims covered by the reporting requirement.

Cf. Comm'r of Internal Rev. v. Clark, 489 U.S. 726, 739 (1989) ("In construing provisions . . . in which a general statement of policy is qualified by an exception, we usually read the exception narrowly in order to preserve the primary operation of the provision.").

Indeed, subsection (d) does not say that the Attorney General may only designate agencies to receive reports for Federal lands and facilities "in which children are cared for or reside." 42 U.S.C. § 13031(d). It simply specifies that the Attorney General "shall designate an agency to receive and investigate" reports for such lands and facilities, saying nothing about what the Attorney General should do with respect to other Federal lands and facilities. Id. And in implementing this authority, the Attorney General has in fact specified reporting locations for all covered professionals who learn of any covered abuse while engaged in their profession or activity on any federal land or facility, not solely abuse connected to lands or facilities where children are cared for or reside. See 28 C.F.R. § 81.2.

The broad reading of the reporting requirement gains further support from two other provisions in the VCAA that unambiguously apply to all federal lands and facilities, not just those where children are cared for or reside. Subsection (e) requires dissemination of a standard written reporting form to "all mandated reporter groups" "[i]n every federally operated (or contracted) facility, and on all Federal lands." 42 U.S.C. § 13031(e). In other words, reporting forms must be disseminated not only to federal lands and facilities where children are cared for or reside, but to all federal lands and facilities. This provision thus appears to presume that mandated reporter groups exist in every federally operated or contracted facility and on all federal lands. This presumption, in turn, strongly suggests that Congress intended to require the reporting of abuse discovered by covered professionals in the course of their covered activities on all federal lands and in all federal facilities, not simply abuse that occurs on the lands and in the facilities where children are cared for or reside.

Subsection (h) embodies a similar premise. That provision, entitled "[t]raining of prospective reporters," requires "periodic training in the obligation to report, as well as in the identification of abused and neglected children," for "[a]ll individuals in the occupations listed in subsection (b)(1) of this section who work on Federal lands, or are employed in federally operated (or contracted) facilities." 42 U.S.C. § 13031(h). Again, this provision appears to assume that all individuals who work in the listed occupations on all federal lands and in all federal facilities—not solely those where children are cared for or reside—might encounter suspected abuse that must be reported. This further suggests that Congress intended to require covered professionals working on all federal lands and in all federal facilities to report suspected abuse, because the across-the-board training requirement otherwise would serve no clear purpose.

The broad reading of the reporting requirement is also consistent with the scope of subsection (b). Subsection (b)'s specific list of relevant professions and activities echoes the mandatory reporter provisions of numerous state laws requiring the reporting of abuse. Compare 42 U.S.C. § 13031(b) (list set forth supra note 1) with Child Welfare Information Gateway, Dep't of Health & Human

Servs., Mandatory Reporters of Child Abuse and Neglect: Summary of State Laws 2 (Apr. 2010) ("Summary of State Laws"), available athttp://www.childwelfare.gov/systemwide/laws_policies/statutes/manda.pdf (last visited Nov. 7, 2012). The reporting requirement, as defined in subsections (a) and (b), focuses on the nature of the covered professional's employment activity, not the place where the child victim is cared for or resides. Indeed, many of the covered professionals—such as film processors, coroners, and ambulance drivers—would likely learn of suspected child abuse in circumstances that provide no indication whether the child victim is cared for or resides on federal lands or in a federal facility.

The VCAA's legislative history also reflects a congressional intent to enact a far-reaching reporting obligation that would protect as many victims of suspected child abuse as possible. Senator Biden, a co-sponsor of the legislation, called it a "sweeping title aimed at mak[ing] our criminal justice system more effective in cracking down on child abusers, and more gentle in dealing with the child abuse victims." 136 Cong. Rec. 36,312 (1990); see also id. at 16,240 (statement of Sen. Biden) ("[Y]ou, the innocent bystander, you, the third party, you have a legal obligation to report when you observe or have reason to believe that an abuse of an innocent child takes place."); id. at 16,238 (statement of co-sponsor Sen. Reid) ("A critical step in protecting our children is to identify child victims . . . before it is too late. My proposed bill of rights requires certain professionals to identify who they suspect are victims of abuse and neglect.").

As we recognize above, our interpretation of the statute does not reconcile perfectly all of the statute's parts, specifically subsection (a)'s cross-reference to subsection (d). Read in context, however, we think subsection (d) need not and should not be construed to limit either the scope of the reporting requirement under subsection (a) or the Attorney General's authority to designate agencies to receive the required reports. Such an interpretation would be in marked tension with the breadth of subsection (a)'s terms, the requirements of subsections (e) and (h), the scope of subsection (b), and the general evidence of Congress's intent.

The two additional narrowing constructions we identified also fail to make better sense of the statute than the broad reading we have adopted. We first considered whether the reporting requirement should be limited to situations involving children who had been abused on federal lands or facilities. But under this reading, as under your suggested reading, we would have to conclude that Congress acted to limit the apparently broad reporting requirement set forth in subsection (a) through the oblique mechanism of a cross-reference to subsection (d). What is more, this reading, too, would make it difficult to explain the breadth of the mandated training and provision of forms on all federal lands and in all federal facilities in subsections (e) and (h) and the scope of covered professionals in subsection (b). Further, and significantly, this reading would narrow the class of children whose suspected abuse could give rise to a required report, despite the fact that no provision in the statute—including subsection (d)—addresses the location of the suspected abuse.

We also considered a third alternative reading—one that would require reporting only from covered professionals who engage in the specified professions and activities on federal lands or in federal facilities where children are cared for or may have been abused. This construction, too, would rest on a presumption that Congress intended to limit the scope of the reporting obligation through a single cross-reference to subsection (d). Further, it would be in particularly sharp tension with subsections (e) and (h), which require training and distributing reporting forms on all federal lands and in all federal facilities, not just where children are cared for or reside. This reading would also produce an anomalous result—a professional's obligation to report facts giving reason to suspect that a child unconnected with federal lands or facilities had been abused would turn on the apparently unrelated question whether other children happened to be cared for or reside on the lands or in the facility where the professional works. In our judgment, these difficulties make this interpretation less coherent than the broad reading we have given the statute.

We therefore conclude that the best reading of section 13031 as a whole is that a covered professional is required to report suspected child abuse discovered while engaged in the professions or occupations specified in subsection (b) on federal lands or in federal facilities.[4]

We next consider whether "the mere knowledge that a patient has viewed child pornography [would] trigger a covered professional's duty to report the suspected child abuse, even if he or she does not know the identity of the child or children depicted and has no reason to believe the patient knew their identity." VA Letter at 2.[5] In raising this question, you point to language in a later part of subsection (d) providing that, when reports required by subsection (a) are "received by social services or health care agencies, and involve allegations of sexual abuse, serious physical injury,

[4] This interpretation of the reporting requirement is consistent with the law of most States. "All States, the District of Columbia, [and all U.S. territories] have statutes identifying persons who are required to report child maltreatment under specific circumstances," and, in most States, the list of individuals with reporting obligations closely resembles the list of covered professionals in section 13031. Summary of State Laws at 1-2. In fact, some jurisdictions require all persons, not just certain professionals, to report suspected child abuse. Id. at 3. Thus, many, if not all, covered professionals who learn of suspected child abuse on federal lands or in federal facilities would also be required to report under state laws. Covered professionals should therefore consult relevant state law to ensure that they are fully informed about the scope of their legal reporting requirements.

[5] As we have noted, section 13031(b) subjects a wide range of individuals to the reporting duty of subsection (a), including physicians, pharmacists, school officials, detention facility employees, and commercial film and photo processors. See supranote 1 (quoting 42

U.S.C. § 13031(b)). Those covered professionals thus may learn of possible child abuse from a variety of individuals besides those commonly referred to as "patients." For simplicity, however, we use the term "patient" as shorthand for any person from whom a covered professional may learn of potential child abuse or life-threatening neglect of a child, there shall be an immediate referral of the report to a law enforcement agency with authority to take emergency action to protect the child." 42 U.S.C. § 13031(d) (emphasis added). Based on subsection (d)'s reference to "the" child, you note that, while it is clear that "the [reporting] requirement applies when the identity of an abused child can be determined by the covered provider so that the law-enforcement agency with jurisdiction can be identified, . . . it is less clear . . . that it applies when that is not the case." VA Letter at 2.6We conclude, however, that the text of the statute covers the situation you describe.

The text of subsection 13031(a) imposes a reporting duty on a covered professional "who, while engaged in a professional capacity or activity described in subsection (b) learns of facts that give reason to suspect that a child has suffered an incident of child abuse." 42 U.S.C. § 13031(a). "[C]hild abuse," in turn, is defined as "the physical or mental injury, sexual abuse or exploitation, or negligent treatment of a child." Id. § 13031(c)(1). The statute further provides that "the term 'sexual abuse' includes the employment [or] use . . . of a child to engage in . . . sexual exploitation of children," and that "the term 'exploitation' means child pornography or child prostitution." Id. § 13031(c)(4)-(6). Under these definitions, covered professionals must report suspected abuse if they learn of facts giving reason

6. Similarly, the Department of Defense states that its relevant policy "does not contemplate that the statute applies in a situation where the patient merely blurts out that he has an addiction to child pornography." Instead, under its policy, reporting would be required in contexts where the patient "is drawn to a particular child," "knows the identity or whereabouts of a child depicted in the pornography," "help[s] to produce the pornography," or in other contexts where

"there is an identifiable child or identifiable children that could be the subject of action by the child protective agency." E-mail for Jeannie S. Rhee, Deputy Assistant Attorney General, Office of Legal Counsel, from John Casciotti, Office of General Counsel, Dep't of Defense (Feb. 26, 2010 5:02 PM). The Department of State "does not have a formal position or policy addressing whether the reporting requirement is triggered when a covered professional learns that someone has viewed child pornography, but the professional does not know the identity of the child or children depicted and has no reason to believe that the viewer knows their identities." E-mail for Jeannie S. Rhee, Deputy Assistant Attorney General, Office of Legal Counsel, from Robert Choo, Office of the Legal Adviser, Dep't of State (July 21, 2010 2:35 PM). It recognizes, however, that this situation "may trigger other actions including the enforcement of child pornography laws, if applicable, or internal discipline." I'd too suspect that a child "has suffered an incident of [employment or use to engage in child pornography],"7or "has suffered an incident of [child pornography]."

Although section 13031 does not define the term "child pornography," it is defined elsewhere in the U.S. Code as "any visual depiction, . . . whether made or produced by electronic, mechanical, or other means, of sexually explicit conduct, where—(A) the production of such visual depiction involves the use of a minor engaging in sexually explicit conduct; (B) such visual depiction is . . . of a minor engaging in sexually explicit conduct; or (C) such visual depiction has been created, adapted, or modified to appear that an identifiable minor is engaging in sexually explicit conduct." 18 U.S.C. § 2256(8) (2006).8This definition is consistent with dictionary definitions of child pornography. See, e.g., Black's Law Dictionary1279 (9th ed. 2009) (defining "child pornography" as "[m]aterial depicting a person under the age of 18 engaged in sexual activity").

Under these definitions, child pornography is not a specific action or set of actions, but an end product, a particular kind of visual depiction that is "made or produced." 18 U.S.C. § 2256(8).

It is thus not entirely clear what it means "to engage in child pornography," or for "a child" to have "suffered an incident of" child pornography. Notably, however, certain other forms of "child abuse"

7. The substitution in the text is not completely straightforward, in that the statute defines "exploitation"—without any qualification—to include "child pornography or child prostitution," but defines "sexual abuse" to include "rape, molestation, prostitution, or other form[s] of sexual exploitation of children." Compare42 U.S.C. § 13031(c)(6) (definition of "exploitation") with id. § 13031(c)(4) (definition of "sexual abuse"). We do not think, however, that the statute intends to draw a strong distinction between "exploitation" and "sexual exploitation." The latter phrase is not a defined term. And the statute in other respects seems to treat the two terms as essentially interchangeable. In particular, the definition of "sexual abuse" expressly provides that "prostitution of children" is a form of "sexual exploitation of children," and the definition "exploitation" similarly provides that "child prostitution" is a form of exploitation." Id.§ 13031(c)(4)-(6).

8Other definitions in section 13031, including the definition of "sexually explicit conduct"—a concept closely related to "child pornography," as the definition quoted above makes clear—track definitions in the same section (chapter 110) of the criminal code. Compare

42 U.S.C. § 13031(c)(5) (2006) with18 U.S.C. § 2256(2) (2006). in section 13031 are also defined as end results rather than actions. [P]hysical injury," for example, is defined to include, among other things, "lacerations, fractured bones, burns, [and] internal injuries." 42 U.S.C. § 13031(c)(2). And it is relatively straightforward to conclude that a child has "suffered an incident of" lacerations or fractured bones if the child has been subjected to physical abuse that results in those injuries. We think it is similarly clear that, whatever else the phrase may include, a person has "engage[d] in child pornography" if that person has produced or created pornographic images of children, and that "a child has suffered an incident of" child pornography if that child has been made the subject of pornographic

images. The pornography is "a permanent record" of the abusive conduct of creating a pornographic image of a child. See New York v. Ferber, 458U.S. 747, 759 (1982).

Based on this analysis, we conclude that a covered professional who learns that a patient under his or her care has viewed child pornography may be aware of "facts that give reason to suspect that a child"—the subject of the specific pornographic images viewed by the patient—"has suffered an incident of child abuse." 42 U.S.C. § 13031(a).

We do not believe a covered professional in such a situation is relieved of an obligation to report such facts simply because he or she does not know or have reason to know or have reason to believe a patient knows, the identity of the child depicted in the pornography. Section 13031(a) and (d) does not require, either expressly or by implication, that a covered professional (or his or her patient) know the identity of the child or children abused in order to have a reporting obligation. We generally "'resist reading words or elements into a statute that do not appear on its face.'" Dean v. United States, 556 U.S. 568, 572 (2009) (quoting Bates v. United States, 522 U.S. 23, 29 (1997)). Moreover, imposing a requirement that the victim's identity be known would be in tension with Congress's protective purpose. See e.g.,136 Cong. Rec. at 36,312 (noting that the statute would "make [the] criminal justice system more effective in cracking down on child abusers").

Even assuming that the statute's references to "a child" in section 13031(a) and (d) limit the reporting requirement to situations involving "a" specific, potentially identifiable child, that limitation provides no basis for imposing the additional prerequisites to reporting that the covered professional know or have reason to believe his or her patient knows the identity of a child depicted in pornography the patient admits to viewing. Pornography may well involve "a" specific, potentially identifiable child even if neither covered professionals nor their patients know the child's identity. Even if covered professionals (or their patients) do not know the identity of any children depicted in pornography viewed by a patient, a report may lead authorities to specific, identifiable children. While some child pornography may be the work of professionals and therefore difficult to link to specific identifiable children, other such images are homemade recordings, taken in domestic contexts, of sexually abusive acts "committed against young neighbors or family members," and therefore traceable through law enforcement investigation to a particular child or children. Philip Jenkins, Beyond Tolerance: Child Pornography on the Internet82 (2001); see also Richard Wortley & Stephen Smallbone, Cmty. Oriented Policing Servs., Dep't of Justice, Problem-Oriented Guides for Police, Problem-Specific Guides Series No. 41, Child Pornography on the Internet 9 (2006), available athttp://www.cops.usdoj.gov/Publications/e04062000.pdf (last visited Nov. 7, 2012) ("[M]ore commonly, amateurs make records of their own sexual abuse exploits, particularly now that electronic recording devices such as digital cameras and web cams permit individuals to create high quality, homemade images.").

For the same reasons, section 13031(d)'s statement that, in certain circumstances, social services or health care agencies must refer reports of suspected child abuse "to a law enforcement agency with authority to take emergency action to protect the child," 42 U.S.C. § 13031(d) (emphasis added), should not be read to restrict the reporting obligation to situations in which covered professionals know the identity of the children who are the victims of suspected abuse. This law-enforcement referral requirement applies not to covered professionals, but to the "social services or health care agencies" that receive reports of suspected child abuse. Id. The statute expressly contemplates that the agency receiving the report, not the covered professional, must ascertain which law enforcement agency is "authori[zed] to take emergency action to protect the child." Id. And although the referral requirement could be read to reflect an assumption that these agencies generally will know the identity of the child in need of protection, the requirement also could be satisfied by identifying a law enforcement agency with authority to initiate an investigation to ascertain the identity and location of the suspected victim.

We therefore conclude that the fact that a patient has viewed child pornography may constitute a "fact[] that give[s] reason to suspect that a child has suffered an incident of child abuse" under section 13031, and that a covered professional is not relieved of the obligation to report such a fact simply because the identity of the injured child is unknown.

C.

As noted, the VCAA provides for criminal penalties. 18 U.S.C. § 2258. When interpreting a statute's civil provision, the violation of which is also subject to criminal sanction, the rule of lenity may be invoked to resolve ambiguity in the provision. See Leocal v. Ashcroft, 543 U.S. 1, 11-12 & n.8 (2004); United States v. Thompson/Center Arms Co., 504 U.S. 505, 517-18 & n.10 (1992) (plurality opinion). Here, however, we resolved both of the interpretive questions you presented without employing the rule of lenity, because we concluded that the provisions at issue did not present any "grievous ambiguity or uncertainty" that could not be addressed by applying ordinary tools of statutory construction. Muscarello v. United States, 524 U.S. 125, 139 (1998) (internal quotation marks and citations omitted).

We recognize, however, that the statutory trigger for the reporting requirement—the learning of "facts that give reason to suspect that a child has suffered an incident of child abuse"—is extremely broad. For example, the statute's text does not appear to require either that the suspected abuse have occurred recently or that there be a direct connection between the facts and a particular perpetrator of or witness to abuse. Thus, a doctor's duty to report conceivably could be triggered by a patient's revelation that his neighbor confided that he was abused as a child some decades ago, a patient's revelation that acquaintances long ago had viewed child pornography, or a patient's expression of amazement that he had learned from the Internet that child abuse or child pornography was far more prevalent than he had previously believed.

9 Because failures to report may be criminally prosecuted, courts may be concerned about the uncertain breadth of the suspected abuse

that may be subject to section 13031's reporting requirement, particularly when combined with the ambiguities discussed in Parts II.A and II.B.

You have not asked us to define the boundaries of the phrase "facts that give reason" to suspect child abuse or to discuss the application of 18 U.S.C. § 2258, but we note that covered professionals who fail to make a report required by the statute may not always be criminally liable for their failure to do so. Significantly, although the VCAA's criminal penalty provision lacks an express mens rea requirement, courts generally "interpret[]criminal statutes to include broadly applicable scienter requirements, even where the statute by its terms does not contain them." X-Citement Video, Inc., 513 U.S. at 70.10Courts deciding whether to impose criminal penalties on a covered professional for failing to file a report would have to decide (i) whether to construe 18 U.S.C. § 2258 to impose a mens rea requirement, and (ii) if they do so, what the required mens rea is. And while for some statutes, courts have required only that a defendant have knowledge of the "facts that make his conduct illegal," Staples, 511 U.S. at 605, for others, courts have required that a defendant know that his or her conduct was "unauthorized or illegal" before criminal liability could be imposed, particularly where

9. We do not consider here whether other aspects of the language quoted in the text above, or of language elsewhere in the statute, might limit its application in some such situations. A court might also adopt a narrowing construction of the statutory trigger for the reporting requirement to avoid notice concerns. See Skilling v. United States, 130 S. Ct. 2896, 2931 (2010).

10. As the Supreme Court has explained, the presumption that a statute contains a mens rea requirement even when that requirement is not explicit in the statutory text is consistent with the rule of lenity. See Liparota v. United States, 471 U.S. 419, 427-28 (1985). Inferring a mens rea requirement is, however, a distinct practice from applying the rule of lenity, and the Court has suggested that lenity principles may not apply in determining the degree of mens rea that is required. See Staples v. United States, 511 U.S. 600, 619 n.17

(1994). failure to impose such a requirement would "criminalize a broad range of apparently innocent conduct." Liparota v. United States, 471 U.S. 419, 426, 434 (1985). Here, a court concerned about ordinary citizens' ability to decipher the contours of the abuse that must be reported, or about the statute's punishment of a failure to act rather than an affirmative act, might be inclined to adopt this kind of heightened mens rea requirement.

See Skilling, 130 S. Ct. at 2927-28 (noting that a "'criminal offense'" must be defined "'with sufficient definiteness that ordinary people can understand what conduct is prohibited'") (quoting Kolender v. Lawson, 461 U.S. 352, 357 (1983)); id. at 2933 (noting that a "mens rea requirement" can help "blunt[] . . . notice concern[s]"); Lambert v. California, 355 U.S. 225, 228 (1957) (holding that due process requires that a person who is "wholly passive and unaware of any wrongdoing" must have notice of a registration requirement before she may be held criminally liable).

III.

In sum, any person who, while engaged in a professional capacity or activity described in subsection (b) of section 13031 on any federal land or in any federally operated (or contracted) facility, learns of "facts that give reason to suspect that a child has suffered any incident of child abuse" must report the suspected abuse to a designated agency. The fact that a patient has viewed child pornography may "give reason to suspect that a child has suffered an incident of child abuse" under the statute, and a covered professional is not relieved of an obligation to report the possible abuse simply because neither the covered professional nor the patient knows the identity of the child depicted in the pornography. As described, however, a covered professional's failure to file a required report will not necessarily result in criminal liability.

VIRGINIA A. SEITZ
Assistant Attorney General
Office of Legal Counsel

A7

Department of Education Title IX Guidelines

Primary guidelines for Title IX are too large to print here. Please refer to http://www2.ed.gov/about/offices/list/ocr/docs/qa-201404-title-ix.pdf for information regarding school requirements and obligations.

A8

PROPOSED PRETRIAL DIVERSION DOCUMENTS

UNITED STATES ATTORNEY
WESTERN DISTRICT OF KENTUCKY
PRETRIAL DIVERSION AGREEMENT

John W. Smith

_____(Address of Defendant)

_____

_____(Defendant Phone No.)

Case No. 3:14-CR-99-JHM

It appearing that you have committed an offense against the United States, in that on or about February 12, 2013, you failed to report to social services or law enforcement facts that gave you reason to suspect a child had suffered an incident of child abuse, and it further appearing, after an investigation of the offense, and of your background, that the interest of the United States and your own interest will be served by deferring prosecution of the matter, in accordance with the following procedure:

On authority of the Attorney General of the United States, by John E. Kuhn, Jr., Acting United States Attorney for the Western District of Kentucky, prosecution in this District for this offense shall be diverted for the period of 12 months from this date, provided you abide by the following conditions:

(1) You shall refrain from violation of any law (federal, state and local). You shall immediately contact your Probation Officer if arrested or questioned by a law enforcement officer.

(2) You shall complete 50 hours of community service prior to the end of the 12-month period of this Pretrial Diversion Agreement. You shall provide your Probation Officer with proof of completion of these community service hours.

(3) You shall make a payment of $100 in restitution prior to or at the execution of this agreement.

(4) You shall follow the Probation Officer's instructions and advice.

(5) You shall report to the Probation Officer as directed.

During the period of pretrial diversion, the United States Attorney may:

(1) Revoke or modify any condition of this deferred prosecution;

(2) Change the period of supervision;

(3) Discharge you from supervision;

(4) Proceed with your prosecution for this offense if you violate these conditions.

If you comply with these conditions during the period of supervision, the United States Attorney will not pursue any further criminal prosecution against you in this district for any offense described in this agreement, and any charges filed for any offense described in this agreement will be dismissed with prejudice.

JOHN E. KUHN, JR.
Acting United States Attorney

_____

Amanda E. Gregory
Assistant U. S. Attorney

_____

Date

Divertee Waiver

I assert and acknowledge that the Sixth Amendment to the Constitution of the United States provides that in all criminal prosecutions the accused shall enjoy the right to a speedy and public trial. I also am aware that Rule 48(b) of the Federal Rules of Criminal Procedure provides that the Court may dismiss an indictment, information, or complaint for unnecessary delay in presenting a charge to the grand jury, filing an information or in bringing a defendant to trial. I hereby request the United States Attorney for the Western District of Kentucky to defer prosecution of the offenses described in this agreement. I agree and consent that any delay from the date of this agreement to the date of trial, as provided for in the terms expressed herein, shall be deemed to be a necessary delay at my request, and I waive any defense to such prosecution on the ground that such delay operated to deny my rights under Rule 48(b) of the Federal Rules of Criminal Procedure and the Sixth Amendment to the Constitution of the United States to a speedy trial or to bar the prosecution by reason of the running of the statute of limitations for a period of months equal to the period of this agreement.

I further understand and agree that the Speedy Trial Act, at 18 U.S.C. Sec. 3161(h)(2), allows exclusion of any delay between the filing of an information or indictment and trial when prosecution is deferred pursuant to this written pretrial diversion agreement for the purpose of allowing me to demonstrate good conduct. I will join in filing an Agreed Order requesting that the Court continue all further criminal proceedings, including trial, and requesting such Court approval as may be necessary to allow me to participate in Pretrial Diversion and to exclude any such delay from the Speedy Trial Act calculations, if criminal charges are filed against me by information or indictment.

I hereby state that I have read and understand the above Pretrial Diversion Agreement and Divertee Waiver. I understand the charges that have been or could be filed against me, and I understand the conditions of my pretrial diversion and agree that I will comply with them.

_____

_____

Defendant Date

_____

_____

Defense Counsel Date

I will accept supervision of the above-named individual.

_____

_____

U.S. Probation Officer Date

A9

Memorandum of Agreement between Fort Knox and the Kentucky Department of Child Based Services (DCBS)

MEMORANDUM OF UNDERSTANDING
BETWEEN
US ARMY GARRISON, FORT KNOX, KENTUCKY
AND
KENTUCKY CABINET FOR HEALTH AND FAMILY SERVICES
DEPARTMENT FOR COMMUNITY BASED SERVICES
SALT RIVER TRAIL SERVICE REGION
(SHEPHERDSVILLE, KENTUCKY)

SUBJECT: Abuse and Neglect of Children of Military Families

1. PURPOSE. This Memorandum of Understanding (MOU) establishes written procedures to integrate the exercise of authority vested in the Kentucky Cabinet for Health and Family Services, Department for Community Based Services [DCBS] and Fort Knox, Kentucky, in matters involving the abuse and neglect of children of military families. These procedures are to be followed by the Kentucky Cabinet for Health and Family Services, Department for Community Based Services [hereinafter, "DCBS"] and the Fort Knox Family Advocacy Program [hereinafter, "FAP"]. This agreement does not purport to create additional jurisdiction vested in any of the parties. This agreement supersedes all previous agreements between DCBS authorities and Fort Knox pertaining to child abuse and neglect and misconduct.

REFERENCES:

a. AR 608-18, the Army Family Advocacy Program, 30 October 2007.

b. 42 U.S.C. 5101, The Child Abuse Prevention and Treatment Act.

c. Kentucky Revised Statutes [KRS] Chapters 600-645, Unified Juvenile Code.

d. Kentucky Administrative Regulations (KAR) Title 922, Cabinet for Health and Family Services Department for Community Based Services Protection and Permanency.

e. DoD Instruction 4000.19, "Interservice and Interdepartmental Support," August 1995.

2. SCOPE / LIMITATIONS: Fort Knox and The Kentucky Department of Community Based Services mutually agree that the following limits apply to this agreement.

a. That for those children residing on Fort Knox who need protection from child abuse and neglect, to include foster care placement, the laws of the Commonwealth of Kentucky as set forth in Kentucky Revised Statutes [KRS] Unified Juvenile Code and Kentucky Administrative Regulations (KAR) shall apply.

b. That for those children residing off post, but within the Commonwealth of Kentucky, who need protection from child abuse and neglect, the laws of the Commonwealth of Kentucky as set forth in KRS and KAR, relating to juvenile services, shall apply.

c. That Fort Knox and DCBS further agree that the definitions of terms that shall apply to this Memorandum are those set forth in Army Regulation 608-18 and in the KRS Unified Juvenile Code.

d. That the Case Review Committee (CRC) for child abuse and the Department of Social Work Service, Ireland Army Community Hospital, Fort Knox, Kentucky, are the primary organizations responsible for administering this agreement on Fort Knox.

e. It is understood and agreed by and between the parties hereto that the United States Army will not pay or reimburse for services provided by DCBS.

3. DCBS shall perform the following in support of this agreement:

a. Investigate reported cases of child abuse and neglect, on Fort Knox in accordance with the Kentucky Unified Juvenile Code and the Standards of Practice of DCBS.

b. To the extent permitted by law, notify the Family Advocacy Program (FAP) Social Work Service (SWS) of all investigations of suspected or substantiated child abuse and neglect cases involving Army families who are residents of Ft. Knox. DCBS will request support from the FAP as appropriate and will provide pertinent information to FAP for presentation to the CRC. DCBS will report or make information accessible to FAP/SWS on the status of these cases on an as needed basis, including investigative findings.

c. Provide appropriate protective services, including case management services to all active cases, and as appropriate, utilize the CRC as a resource.

d. DCBS or any interested party may file a petition in District/Family Court for the removal of abused and/or neglected children from the home of parents/guardian and regarding the placement of these children per KRS 620.070.

e. Promptly secure emergency protective custody for children determined to be in imminent danger or at risk of serious injury and notify SWS of placement.

f. Whenever possible, coordinate intended visits to installation agencies / units / organizations in advance to arrange necessary cooperation and/or assistance of Fort Knox officials.

4. FORT KNOX shall perform the following in support of this agreement:

a. Immediately report all suspected cases of child abuse and neglect to DCBS Centralized Intake.

b. Provide access to Fort Knox and government housing areas to DCBS social services workers as needed. Such access to housing areas is necessary to investigate and work with families to protect children and to effect the reunification of children who have been removed from their parents' custody.

c. Upon request of a DCBS social worker, provide police escorts for social services workers to specified locations on post.

d. Provide or coordinate medical care/examination for involved children, in accordance with applicable regulations.

e. Coordinate and support the local CRC in accordance with AR 608-18.

f. Encourage individuals with knowledge of suspected cases of child abuse and neglect to report directly to DCBS.

g. Through the CRC, Department of Social Work, Ireland Army Community Hospital, Fort Knox, KY will provide the following:

(1) Notify DCBS of scheduled CRC and /or FAP staff meetings involving mutual child abuse and/or neglect cases.

(2) Support DCBS in all phases of its work on Fort Knox.

(3) Provide assistance to DCBS in evaluating, assessing, and determining an appropriate family services case plan with the family upon request for child abuse and neglect cases and in arranging required treatment services from military and civilian agencies.

(4) Obtain Medical records, background and central registry checks and provide findings to DCBS within twenty-four hours of referral.

(5) Upon request of DCBS, provide documentary and /or testimonial evidence, as required and in accordance with applicable law and regulations, in support of DCBS efforts before the District/Family Court.

(6) Fort Knox will provide access to children in possible need of protection while at on-post schools without prior notification of parents.

5. RESPONSIBILITIES: All Parties agree to the following:

a. Work cooperatively to provide services for abused or neglected children and their families.

b. Utilize the Lincoln Trail Advocacy and Support Center for interviews, counseling and/or medical examinations to the extent practicable and when it is the best interest of the child.

c. Jointly investigate referrals involving allegations of sexual abuse, as dictated by the Kentucky Revised Statutes (KRS).

d. During joint investigation, DCBS will work cooperatively with Ft. Knox Military Police [MPs], Criminal Investigations Division [CID], and/or Provost Marshal [PM].

e. Address day-to-day delivery problems and concerns to their respective inter-agency contact persons. If service delivery or administrative problems cannot be resolved, they will be referred through the respective chain of command for resolution.

f. Review this MOU on an annual basis and recommend any proposed changes to the Garrison Commander, Fort Knox, KY or to the Commissioner of DCBS.

g. This MOU may be amended with the mutual agreement of the parties.

h. This MOU shall be effective upon the signatures of the parties below and will remain in effect until terminated by either party, or their authorized agents, by thirty (30) days written notice.

LIABILITY. DCBS and Fort Knox shall assume responsibility for their own program delivery and conduct of their own staff. Fort Knox will not provide medical care of DCBS employees, except for life-threatening emergencies as outlined in Army Regulation 40-3.

CONFIDENTIALITY. All parties to this agreement agree to abide by all laws and regulations governing the confidentiality of patient information and further agree to vigorously safeguard privileged information in accordance with HIPPA and applicable laws, statutes, ordinances, or regulations.

6. EFFECTIVE DATE: **IN WITNESS WHEREOF**, this Memorandum of Understanding is executed by the parties on this the _50_ day of _June_____, 2010.

ERIC C. SCHWARTZ
COL, AR
Garrison Commander

RONALD J. PLACE
COL, MC
Hospital Commander

PATRICIA R. WILSON
COMMISSIONER
Department for Community Based Services
Kentucky Cabinet for Health and Family Services

F. RYAN KEITH
GENERAL COUNSEL
Kentucky Cabinet for Health and Family Services

A10

FINAL PRETRIAL PRESS RELEASE FROM DISTRICT ATTORNEY

FOR IMMEDIATE RELEASE
Friday, August 28, 2015
Former Police Officer And School Administrator Pleads Guilty To
Violating Sex Abuse Laws

LOUISVILLE, Ky. – A Grayson County, Kentucky, former police
officer and school administrator pleaded guilty in U.S. District Court
to violating federal and state sex abuse laws, announced United States
Attorney John E. Kuhn, Jr.

Stephen E. Miller, age 45, pleaded guilty to four counts in
superseding information, on July 30, 2015, and this week Chief
Judge Joseph H. McKinley, Jr. accepted the plea and scheduled sentencing for November 2, 2015 at 11:00am in Louisville.

Miller pleaded guilty to engaging in abusive sexual contact with
three female students and third degree sodomy with a fourth female

student. The incidents occurred at Bluegrass Challenge Academy between February and August 2013.

Miller previously worked as a police officer in Leitchfield, Kentucky. He resigned the position following complaints of inappropriate conduct toward two women. Miller then began working at Bluegrass Challenge Academy, a residential, educational program run by the Kentucky National Guard, located on Fort Knox Military Base. Miller had supervisory authority over the Academy students.

Miller faces a maximum sentence of 11 years in prison, a fine of up to $1,000,000 and at least five years of supervised release. John Smith, who was the director of Bluegrass Challenge Academy during the time, has been indicted for failure to report child abuse. If convicted, he faces a maximum sentence of one year in prison, a fine of up to $100,000, and up to one year of supervised release.

Assistant United States Attorneys Amanda E. Gregory and Stephanie M. Zimdahl are prosecuting the case. The Federal Bureau of Investigation (FBI) with assistance from the Army Criminal Investigation Division conducted the investigation.

A11

DEFENDANT'S SENTENCING MEMORANDUM

UNITED STATES DISTRICT COURT
WESTERN DISTRICT OF KENTUCKY
AT LOUISVILLE

CRIMINAL ACTION NO. 3:14CR-99-JHM
UNITED STATES OF AMERICA PLAINTIFF

vs.

JOHN W. SMITH   DEFENDANT

<u>DEFENDANT'S SENTENCING MEMORANDUM</u>

Comes the defendant, by counsel, and for his sentencing memorandum herein states as follows:

Mr. Smith was convicted at trial of one (1) count of failure to report child abuse in violation of 18 U.S.C. § 2258. The original Presentence Report [hereinafter referred to as "PSR"] calculates Mr.

Smith's total offense level for the charge as 6 and his criminal history as I, for an advisory sentencing range of zero to six months incarceration, does not require any probation, and indicates a guideline fine level of $500 to $5000.

For the reasons set herein below, the defense respectfully requests the Court sentence the defendant to a minimal probationary period, community service as the Court deems necessary, a fine of $100.00, and that he be held harmless in relation to the restitution requested by the United States.

Statement of Background

Bluegrass ChalleNGe Academy ("BCA") is one of two Kentucky Youth ChalleNGe programs. Youth ChalleNGe is a national "quasi-military" program established by 32 U.S.C. § 509, operating in many states under supervisory control of the Department of Defense, Assistant Secretary of Defense for Reserve Affairs; the National Guard Bureau, Office of Athletics and Youth Development; and through Cooperative Agreement with the Commonwealth of Kentucky, Department of Military Affairs. The Master Youth Program Cooperative Agreement, supplemented by policy memoranda, define the requirements and responsibilities of all programs. As such, Section 803 of this cooperative agreement identifies Youth ChalleNGe Programs as Title IX programs.

These programs exist for the voluntary attendance of 16 – 18 years old applicants who have dropped out of high school, are at risk of dropping out, and have demonstrated inclinations for involvement within the courts. However, it should be noted that no applicant with a felony conviction may be considered for routine acceptance and no child can be court ordered to attend Youth ChalleNGe. The program is an 18-month program, with 22-weeks of residential training and a one-year post residential period under the supervision of a family nominated, program trained mentor. Applicants complete a rigorous application and acceptance effort, providing personal history, medical history, criminal history, a mentor nomination and, if conditionally accepted, must finally complete an entrance physical before final acceptance. Cadets are required to be drug free during the program. The program provides a rigorous training schedule, enforcing seven core components. The program uses the military structural model without any martial aspect of training. BCA incorporated high school credit recovery with the traditional GED educational component. The program contracts with Fort Knox Schools to provide meals and snacks in accordance with School Lunch Program guidelines. Carbonated and caffeinated beverages are discouraged along with high sugar snacks. Cadets earn limited privileges for these items as they progress through the program. All cadets are expected to maintain personal clothing, maintain high personal hygiene standards and in the case of male cadets, to shave every morning. All these elements instill good time management and hygiene habits in BCA graduates. Cadets are encouraged to write letters to parents and friends, both as a means of traditional contact and to increase writing skills for their classes. Cell phones are not allowed and calls are limited to weekends until cadets achieve Level III status. At Level III status, they have additional privileges for calls. Cadets are monitored to insure they do not exceed the allotted times for calls and to insure that they do not use loud and/or inappropriate language with their parents. Cost of calls is paid for by the program as past phone card practices indicated families wasted much money when a cadet reached an answering machine at home. Cadets are encouraged to participate in a variety of sporting activities including basketball, softball, volleyball, and archery.

Mr. Smith served as Director of BCA from June 2003 until December 2013. As Director, he developed a Management Team consisting of the Deputy, the Commandant, the Budget Analyst/EEOC, the Information Management Officer, the Operations and Logistics Supervisor, and the Lead Instructor. Occasionally, the Platoon Sergeants were included in these meetings. All Cadre and Cadets were under the supervision of the Commandant and the Platoon Sergeants. The program followed guidance from the Master Youth Programs Cooperative Agreement, Commonwealth of Kentucky, and Department of Military Affairs guidance. The contractual agreement allowing BCA to operate on Fort Knox was signed by the leadership of the Fort Knox Army Garrison, the Adjutant General of Kentucky, and the United States Property and Fiscal Officer. All management and operations policy came from the Department of Military Affairs and through message traffic from the National Guard Bureau.

In early-February 2013, the teacher (Stewart) working with the female platoon was notified by another cadet that other cadets were discussing filing a 'sexual harassment' complaint against the Platoon Supervisor (SM). Upon hearing this, the teacher contacted the Platoon Assistant Supervisor (Onusko) and the two of them interviewed cadets named in the report individually. Immediately after interviewing the cadets, Onusko took the notes from the interviews to the Commandant (Burgess) to report the situation. Upon reading the notes, Burgess immediately prepared a formal request to the Equal Employment Opportunity Commission (EEOC) (Graves) representative to conduct an investigation. This request was transmitted to the EEOC and to Mr. Smith (at home on his regular day off) electronically. Ms. Graves had taken the afternoon off to accomplish personal business after being made aware of the situation came to BCA on Saturday to begin the EEOC (and Title IX) sexual harassment investigation. Mr. Smith arrived at BCA the following Monday morning and received a preliminary briefing from Burgess (who was only aware of allegations made). Mr. Smith knocked and entered Graves's office to find her in the middle of an interview. He apologized and departed. Upon noticing the cadet leave the room, Smith entered Graves's office to inquire about a financial report that was due. After clearing that information, Graves wanted to share what she had found regarding the investigation to date. Other than Burgess' report, this briefing was the first knowledge Mr. Smith had regarding the investigation. Burgess had led Mr. Smith to think the problem was widespread within the platoon; however, Graves provided a more accurate estimate of the situation. It was during this meeting that Smith learned there were two complainants. During this meeting, Graves expressed her comments that the allegations were basically 'She said, He said' with no clear means to determine the truth. When pressed regarding other investigative opportunities, Mr. Smith recommended Graves review the classroom camera footage as one of the incidents was alleged to have occurred in the classroom. Graves indicated she would begin that immediately. Mr. Smith told Ms. Graves to complete the investigation and decide what she felt the evidence pointed to. Ms Graves later reported viewing video segments in the classroom for multiple full days and saw no indication that SM was ever behind the cadet who alleged he 'rubbed himself on her shoulder.' When confronted with this evidence, the cadet recanted and indicated that he 'just got too close to her'. Graves indicated the only time Miller's body might have touched the cadet was when he sat beside her to assist with a classroom problem. She indicated 'his knee may have touched her knee, if anything touched at all.' After viewing the video of the second incident, Graves notices SM and DM entering the Cadre Office (not the supervisor's office) on the third floor, while all the other cadets waited to depart for the evening meal. She indicated that several of the other female cadets were walking to and fro in the hallway looking through the open door. She noticed Platoon Sergeant Windom was on the floor and was positioned in the hallway looking into the office for some time prior to DM departing. Upon seeing this, Graves later interviewed Windom who indicated she saw nothing inappropriate, nor was Cadet DM distressed in any way when she departed the office. Graves ascertained the same demeanor from watching the video. From all the interviews, the video evidence she viewed, and from the observed demeanor of all parties, Graves verbally reported to Mr. Smith she felt any 'contact, if contact occurred, was accidental'. Graves indicated she felt that the potential for future allegations was great unless SM realized that he must allow available female staff and cadre to care for cadets uniforms. Graves then prepared her report and briefed parties, IAW Kentucky Department of Military Affairs ("DMA") and Title IX policy, obtaining acceptance of the recommendations by all parties. After obtaining these acceptances and to further impress upon SM that his actions must involve female staff and cadre more often, Graves brought the parties to the Director's office. Mr. Smith confirmed that all parties agreed to the recommendations, confirmed that parties were aware of their unlimited right to appeal the report, and asked if all recommendations were completed.

Graves indicated the 'reprimand' had not been completed at that time. Mr. Smith directed that it be accomplished before the end of the day and excused all parties.

Mr. Smith, at this juncture, had no reason to suspect that any 'child abuse' had occurred. The contact was reported as accidental—IF contact even occurred. All parties accepted the recommendations of the EEOC who a veteran investigator with over 10 years of experience conducting investigations for BCA and occasionally for DMA at other sites. Had Mr. Smith suspected 'child abuse' he would have notified the Fort Knox CID at that time just as he had done on instances before this investigation and on an occasion after this incident.

Vulnerable Victim Enhancement

The prosecution has argued for a 2-level increase under Section 3A1.1(b)(1) as Mr. Smith 'should have known' DM was a vulnerable victim. There is no indication Mr. Smith should have known anything of the kind. There is no mention on DM's medical history of any past counseling of any kind. There is only an indication of an ankle injury (without details). During the first month of the program, DM presented herself as a leader among her peers, being recommended by Cadre and Platoon Supervisors for early leadership duties. Roughly one week after the incident in this matter involving SM, DM became 18-years of age and was able to self-terminate from the program at any time. Not only did DM not self-terminate when she became so eligible, her family came to Fort Knox shortly thereafter and celebrated her birthday with a party. During her stay at BCA, DM never asked to talk to the contract counselor (Mr. Bruce Hey) and shook off any suggestion that she do so. DM, per a cadre report, experienced an 'anxiety attack' one evening after returning to the academy from an outing with her mentor. Cadre contacted the mother, who indicated DM had these attacks all the time. Upon returning from the Easter Pass (three days at home, and one of three such passes) DM, when asked about exhibited discomfort, indicated she was 'beaten up' by her boyfriend during the weekend and that she was taken to the hospital and told she probably had 'bruised ribs'. DM was instructed to discuss this with the nurse the next day but she never raised the issue. DM continued to be actively involved in the program and played softball for a team being coached by SM. DM completed the program, though failing to score high enough on the Official Practice Test (OPT) to attempt her GED. DM graduated as a Level III, the highest level in the academy. Just before graduation DM named SM as that staff or cadre having the most positive impact during her stay at the academy. From related information, DM did not mention the investigation to her parents. Additionally, a statement from her previous boyfriend indicates she never raised any mention of any inappropriate behavior—rather, only talking about her accomplishments at the academy. Only after graduating and being notified by the FBI of the current investigation did DM seek counseling.

The point is: What evidence indicates Mr. Smith 'should have known' DM was a vulnerable victim? Mr. Smith spent four days each week at the academy starting each by helping keep order in the hall while morning medications were distributed. During this time he discussed many issues, aspirations, and achievements with male and female cadets. There was never any instance where Mr. Smith considered DM vulnerable and no evidence to support a contention that he should have considered her vulnerable. Therefore, any level increase due to DM being a vulnerable victim should be rejected.

Offense Level Considerations

Mr. Smith's total offense level in this case should remain at Level 6. The defense concurs with the prosecution's criminal history score of 0 and a Criminal History Category of I. Mr. Smith is retired. Mr. Smith serves his church as a Deacon, Moderator, Adult Sunday School Teacher, Pastor Search Committee Chairperson and on other church committees. Mr. Smith serves his community as a member of a non-profit Lions Club Treasurer, having served twice previously as President. Mr. Smith provides support to his community through continued works to support city events. COL (Ret) Smith served 28 years in the Kentucky National Guard, 21 of which were on active federal service for the Guard, commanding a Field Artillery Battalion in combat in Operation Desert Storm, leading the Kentucky Military Academy during the implementation of the United States Army Total Army Schools System and ending his career as the Chief of Staff for the Kentucky National Guard. There is absolutely no indication of other than exemplary service and behavior in his record and his offense level should remain at Level 6.

Objection to Restitution Requested by the United States

Mr. Smith, for the reasons expressed above, feels restitution regarding any medical treatment by DM that occurred 18-months after her graduation and 12-months after his retirement is inappropriate. There is not valid evidence that any of the care indicated by the cryptic Explanation of Benefits ("EOB") provided by the United States following trial resulted from any action associated with Mr. Smith. There has been no description of any medical services where Mr. Smith's name was ever mentioned by DM regarding the treatment rendered. Rather, as indicated by the inclusion of x-ray and brain scan billings in the EOBs provided, there seems to be an expressed consideration by the medical professionals that some physical abnormality was considered and had to be either confirmed or ruled out. Absent a review of the therapeutic counseling notes, there can be no correlation between Mr. Smith's actions in this case and the treatment claimed by DM.

Further, it should be noted that the other five (5) misdemeanor co-defendants were required by the United States to pay the sum of $100.00 towards the requested restitution in this matter. Given Mr. Smith is clearly similarly situated with these defendants, there is no logical reason his restitution should be any greater than the restitution paid by these individuals.

Statutory Factors to Consider

As this Court is aware, 18 U.S.C. § 3553(a) sets forth the seven factors that a sentencing court must consider. Each will be stated and then addressed in relation to this case.

1) *The nature and circumstances of the offense and the history and characteristics of the defendant.* This is clearly a case of omission and not commission. Mr. Smith failed to report an incident of suspected child abuse. He did not commit the child abuse. He did not violate anyone. He did not take advantage of anyone. He failed to act and that was his crime. Therefore, the nature and circumstances of the offense support the minimum punishment in this case. Additionally, the history and characteristics of the defendant clearly support the same. It is safe to say that it would be difficult to bring forward an individual who has a more stellar and impressive history. The sheer number of letters written on his behalf to this Court leave no doubt that his character is beyond reproach. And, Mr. Smith's history is impeccable.

2) *The need for the sentence imposed to reflect the four primary purposes of sentencing i.e. retribution, deterrence, incapacitation, and rehabilitation.* This case does not cry out for any of the four purposes to be satisfied in this matter any further than they have already been satisfied. There is no need for retribution under the facts of this case. The same is true with deterrence. Again, this a case of omission and commission. The same is true with incapacitation. Why would anyone want to incapacitate a person as remarkable as Mr. Smith. And, finally, Mr. Smith is not in need of rehabilitation. As stated below, Mr. Smith is rehabilitating himself every day by continuing to ensure others learn from this case.

3) *The kinds of sentences available.* As the presentence investigation report indicates, Mr. Smith is eligible for probation

in this matter. Therefore, the Court has the authority to simply place Mr. Smith on probation as no minimum sentence is required in this matter by statute.

4) *The sentencing range established through application of the sentencing guidelines and the type of sentences available under the guidelines.* As previously stated, Mr. Smith is clearly eligible for probation under the guidelines. The range is 0 to six months in this case.

5) *Any relevant "policy statements" promulgated by the Commission.* Counsel is unaware of any such policy statements that apply to this case.

6) *The need to avoid unwarranted sentencing disparities among defendants with similar records what have been found guilty of similar conduct.* As the Court is likely aware, a total of six (6) defendants, including Mr. Smith, were charged with one (1) misdemeanor count in this case. The remaining five (5) defendants were offered and accepted diversion. Each performed community service, paid a total of $100, and ultimately had their cases dismissed. While it is true Mr. Smith exercised his constitutional right to go to a jury trial in this matter, no real argument can be made that Mr. Smith is not similarly situated with the misdemeanor co-defendants. Therefore, other than to punish Mr. Smith for exercising his rights under the law, there is no reason Mr. Smith should receive anything other than probation, community service, and a $100.00 fine.

7) *The need to provide restitution to any victims of the offense.* This factor is discussed in detail above and Mr. Smith is prepared to pay restitution should the Court so order the same in this matter.

Mr. Smith's Efforts to Educate Academy Personnel Even While Facing Criminal Charges

Through the process of the criminal proceedings and his efforts to fully understand what happened in the case of DM, Mr.

Smith became aware of the intricacies relating to 18 USC § 2258, 42 USC § 13013, 28 CFR 81.2 and KRS 620.030. In an effort to insure the Kentucky Department of Military Affairs, Bluegrass ChalleNGe Academy (BCA), and Appalachian ChalleNGe Academy (ACA) were aware of these same intricacies and to identify policy to preclude any future violations of law, Mr. Smith selflessly travelled to Frankfort, Kentucky to brief the DMA Executive Director, his assistant, the legal representative of DMA, both academy Directors, the BCA Deputy Director and additional ACA staff on what he had learned during the criminal process. Mr. Smith made a presentation to all in attendance regarding the expectations of existing law and how to ensure compliance therewith. Unfortunately, as far as was determined at this April meeting, no representative of the Attorney General had yet provided either a 'reporting format' or any 'periodic training' to anyone in the academy as contemplated under 42 USC § 13031. During the presentation, Mr. Smith shared that while both academies are mandated to conduct sexual harassment investigations as they may occur in accordance with their Title IX status, they should also immediately report any sexual harassment incident to Kentucky Department of Community Based Services (DCBS) as that agency had been identified as the 'designated agency' during his trial. It was learned that this practice is now being implemented and DCBS has begun complaining because there are now a large number of non-child abuse incidents being reported to them. While at the meeting, Mr. Smith recommended that DCBS field a system capable of producing a date and time stamped reply to any reporting person, whether using computer or smart phone. Additionally, he recommended that all staff members be provided a card with a format for reportable information. It was learned that while the academies were responding to protect staff in this new situation, it was also apparent to Mr. Smith that their Title IX efforts may suffer as BCA indicated it would no longer conduct investigations involving BCA staff. They apparently now intend to request an outside agency to conduct any investigation of any incident alleged against a staff. Additional consideration discussed were the discrepancies between 18 USC § 2258, 42 USC § 13031, and KRS 620.030. While federal law involves 'covered professionals', Kentucky law involves 'any person'. In the end analysis, the ability of Fort Knox to assimilate any state charge for federal prosecution means that all persons on Fort Knox are susceptible to indictment, and therefore, must be trained and provided reporting formats.

As discussed above, Mr. Smith's continued efforts to educate others is remarkable. It is safe to assume that the Court rarely experiences individuals who take a criminal conviction and decide to take that negative experience to educate others. This is truly what Mr. Smith has done in this case. He has taken what he has learned and instead of letting it dissuade his efforts to help others, he has used it to help ensure his case and the lessons learned therein are shared with as many people as possible to avoid the situation he experienced from being encountered in the future.

Conclusion

Based on the foregoing, the defense respectfully requests this Court place Mr. Smith on probation for a minimal period, require him to perform community service as the Court deems necessary, and pay a fine of $100.00. There is no individual more deserving of the Court's consideration than Mr. Smith. Mr. Smith is an impeccable person who has spent his life serving others. His record of service to his community, state, and nation is like no other. He deserves to go on with his life with the minimum punishments allowable under the law.

Respectfully Submitted,

/s/ Darren C. Wolff
DARREN C. WOLFF
2615 Taylorsville Road
Louisville, KY 40205
502-451-3911
Counsel for Defendant

<u>CERTIFICATE</u>

I hereby certify that on May 18, 2016, I electronically filed the foregoing with the clerk of the court by using the CM/ECF system, which will send a notice of electronic filing to the following: Amanda Gregory, Esq., Assistant United States Attorney.

/s/ Darren C. Wolff

ABOUT THE AUTHOR

John Wayne Smith resides in the quiet southern Kentucky town of Smiths Grove. He and LaDonna have lived in Smiths Grove most of their lives, raised a family, and then retired among friends and relatives. John Wayne has served his community as a volunteer fire-fighter then chief of the fire department, as the elementary school PTO president, as a member of the local Lions Club, in multiple officer positions and twice president. He has served on numerous appointed commissions to improve the city and Warren County.

John Wayne Smith has served his country in distinguished military service. He retired from this service as the chief of staff of the Kentucky National Guard. He served as commandant of the Kentucky Military Academy, Fort Knox, Kentucky. He commanded the 1st Battalion, 623rd Field Artillery in Operation Desert Storm, only one of four combat arms National Guard battalions deployed to the wartime theater. During his service, he was awarded the Legion of Merit twice, the Bronze Star, the Meritorious Service Medal multiple times and many other recognitions of honorable and faithful service.

After retiring from military service and building a home, John Wayne Smith was asked to consider continuing his efforts in the Kentucky Youth ChalleNGe effort. After serving as a placement coordinator for a short time, he became the director of Bluegrass ChalleNGe Academy in 2003. He served at-risk youth and their families faithfully for 10.5 years, raising academy graduation rates to levels far in excess of program targets, and helped organize and establish a second Kentucky Youth ChalleNGe program in Appalachia.

In 2014, after his retirement, he and five of his former staff were charged with a federal misdemeanor crime of failure to report child abuse. While no one in the organization was ever informed of this potential offense or trained in any manner regarding its existence, the prosecution was able to obtain a conviction in 2016. This is his story regarding the body of work, the charge, and the multiple reasons this effort goes against all established law. May God grant you insight and understanding as you read this account.

CPSIA information can be obtained
at www.ICGtesting.com
Printed in the USA
LVHW01s0021070218
565576LV00004B/5/P

9 781641 400343